LBJ and McNamara:
The Vietnam Partnership Destined to Fail

"Utilizing his unprecedented access to the record, Peter Osnos has excavated the complex relationship between Lyndon B. Johnson and Robert S. McNamara. Osnos expertly pulls back the curtain, revealing the central role that the character and personalities of these two complicated men played in the decision to escalate the war. We learn something new on almost every page."

—ROBERT K. BRIGHAM,
Shirley Ecker Boskey Professor of History and International Relations, Vassar College, and author of *Reckless: Henry Kissinger and the Tragedy of Vietnam* and *Is Iraq Another Vietnam?*

"LBJ and McNamara is a perceptive treatment of the complex but crucial relationship at the heart of U.S. decision making on Vietnam. Peter Osnos vividly conveys how tragedy defined not just the Vietnam war in popular memory but the relationship between two historic figures of twentieth-century America."

—BRIAN VANDEMARK,
Professor of History, United States Naval Academy, and author of *Road to Disaster: A New History of America's Descent into Vietnam*, and *Kent State: An American Tragedy*

"*LBJ and McNamara: The Vietnam Partnership Destined to Fail* brings to one of history's most-well covered topics new insights and a deeper understanding of Johnson and McNamara than we have ever had. . . . The approaching fifty-year anniversary of the end of the Vietnam debacle offers the right moment to learn anew."

—DANIEL WEISS,
Homewood Professor of the Humanities, Johns Hopkins University; president emeritus of the Metropolitan Museum of Art; and author of *In That Time: Michael O'Donnell and the Tragic Era of Vietnam*

Also by Peter L. W. Osnos

Would You Believe … The Helsinki Accords Changed the World?
(with Holly Cartner)

George Soros: A Life in Full
(editor)

An Especially Good View: Watching History Happen

LBJ and McNamara

The Vietnam Partnership Destined to Fail

LBJ and McNamara

The Vietnam Partnership Destined to Fail

Peter L. W. Osnos

Rivertowns BOOKS
IRVINGTON, NEW YORK

This book is published in association with Platform Books LLC.

Copyright © 2024 by Peter L. W. Osnos. All rights reserved.

Cover design by Maryellen Tseng
Cover image © Everett Collection Historical / Alamy Stock Photo

No part of this book may be used or reproduced by any means, graphic, electronic, or mechanical, including photocopying, recording, taping, or by any information storage retrieval system without the written permission of the publisher, except in the case of brief quotations embodied in critical articles and reviews.

Printed in the United States of America • November 2024 • I

Paperback edition ISBN-13: 978-1-953943-55-2
Ebook edition ISBN-13: 978-1-953943-57-6

LCCN Imprint Name: Rivertowns Books
Library of Congress Control Number: 2024944435

Rivertowns Books are available from all bookshops, other stores that carry books, and online retailers. Visit our website at www.rivertownsbooks.com. Orders and other correspondence may be addressed to:

Rivertowns Books
240 Locust Lane
Irvington NY 10533
Email: info@rivertownsbooks.com

Book design by Maryellen Tseng
Set in 12-point Adobe Caslon Pro

*To those on the Vietnam Wall on the Mall
and their countless Vietnamese counterparts.
It did not have to happen.*

Contents

★ ★ ★

Origins	xi
Introduction	1
1– The Kennedy Years	19
2– The Accidental President	49
3– Escalation 1965	69
4– Disillusion and Delusion	91
5– The Breaking Point	104
6– Departure and Beyond	128
Epilogue	137
Sources and Acknowledgments	143
Index	149

Origins

★ ★ ★

This book is the result of more than fifty years of engagement with the subject of conflicts in Indochina, particularly the one that came to be captioned the "American war" in Vietnam from the early 1960s until 1975.

As an assistant to I. F. Stone at his weekly newsletter when escalation began in 1965, as a correspondent based in Saigon for the *Washington Post* between 1970 and 1973, and then through decades of publishing books on the topic, by journalists, veterans, scholars, and most significantly, Robert McNamara's explanatory memoir, *In Retrospect: The Tragedy and Lessons of Vietnam,* I was immersed in the history, the reality as I witnessed it, and the consequences of this twentieth-century war—a ground, air, and propaganda battle that differed from the global conflicts of World Wars I and II.

As an editor at Random House and its imprint Times Books, I also published the memoirs of Clark Clifford, *Counsel to the President,* and Anatoly Dobrynin's *In Confidence: Moscow's Ambassador to America's Six Cold War Pres-*

idents. Those books and my experience working with the authors are also reflected in the narrative. The historian Brian VanDeMark worked closely with both McNamara and Clifford as well as with me on their respective memoirs; his own book *Road to Disaster: A New History of America's Descent into Vietnam* was invaluable as a resource.

Robert Brigham, the Shirley Ecker Boskey Professor of History and International Relations at Vassar College and the author of several highly regarded books on the Vietnam war and its aftermath, shared documentary material from his extraordinary archive of research and fact-checked this narrative. Brigham also worked with McNamara on other Vietnam-related projects and provided essential perspective on how the policy debates evolved and how the personalities of those involved had an impact.

Although I was the editor and publisher of McNamara, Clifford, and Dobrynin, my role was also as a journalist, eliciting their detailed accounts of events and where possible their personal and emotional responses on how they felt the impact. In writing this book, I have sought to blend personal experience, journalism, and scholarship. I think of it as history written by a journalist who was there.

It was McNamara for whom a memoir carried the greatest burden. He was so closely identified with the war and subject to so much criticism that he recognized his book would receive intense scrutiny and public judgment of its contents.

In the course of drafting the manuscript, McNamara

sat down for a series of recorded discussions to elicit deeper responses to the central questions of his time as Lyndon Johnson's secretary of defense. Also participating in these conversations were my editorial colleague Geoff Shandler and McNamara's coauthor, Brian VanDeMark.

Quotations from those sessions appear in the text in italics, and audio from these discussions is available at www.platformbooksllc.net.

In one of these first extended sessions in 1993, McNamara said to me:

I want you to know this—you don't have to act on it—but I have said if, when I finish this, I don't think it's going to be what I call constructive—which means non-self-serving, non-whitewashed, contributing to—I'll call it healing the wounds—I'm going to tear up the contract. I'll pay back the advance and I won't publish. But that's exactly...

To which I replied: *I respect that. I don't think that will happen.*

The book's publication in the spring of 1995 was a major national news story, and the coverage of McNamara's reflections was harsh. A *New York Times* editorial on April 12, was scathing:

> Perhaps the only value of "In Retrospect" is to remind us never to forget that these were men who in the full hubristic glow of their power would not listen to logical warning or ethical appeal ... [McNamara's] regret

cannot be huge enough to balance the books for our dead soldiers ... Surely he must in every quiet and prosperous moment hear the ceaseless whispers of those poor boys in the infantry, dying in the tall grass, platoon by platoon, for no purpose. What he took from them cannot be repaid by prime-time apology and stale tears, three decades late.

It was of course too late to change or amend McNamara's book with further justifications. Despite the reception, it became a number-one national bestseller. I never heard from McNamara then or ever that he was sorry he had written the book.

As I have reread the reviews after so many years, I see that they all concentrated on what McNamara might have said or done decades earlier, rather than his explanations, a missed opportunity for drawing historical lessons.

★ ★ ★ ★ ★

As the United States approached the fiftieth anniversary of the withdrawal of the last American combat forces from Vietnam, I began to focus on what I have come to believe was a decisive factor in what was, ultimately, an American defeat: the relationship, personalities, and characters of the two men most closely identified with the misbegotten policies, Lyndon Baines Johnson and Robert Strange McNamara.

My work with McNamara, beginning in 1993 and culminating in the publication of *In Retrospect* in 1995, involved scores of conversations that enabled him to confront what went so badly wrong. The hundreds of pages of transcripts, I now realized, were more candid and therefore revealing than what McNamara would allow himself to say in the book.

The release of hundreds of hours of audio recordings from Johnson's presidency, many dealing with Vietnam; the assessment of LBJ prior to the height of the Vietnam war in Robert Caro's monumental biography; and a library of relevant books by others have provided me with the narrative to make the point that the Johnson-McNamara partnership, so crucial to the war, was from the outset destined to end in failure.

And based on their own words, the two men knew that they would certainly not prevail, almost from the moment they began working together on November 22, 1963, the day President John F. Kennedy was assassinated in Dallas.

This book describes what happened in the years between 1963 and McNamara's last day as secretary of defense in February 1968, only weeks before Johnson himself would announce that he would not run for reelection that fall. Johnson returned to Texas by any measure a broken man, and McNamara spent the rest of his life, privately and eventually publicly, coming to terms with the debacle.

This book is an account of how this happened and, to the extent possible, why.

★ ★ ★ ★ ★

This narrative appeared as a series of eighteen installments on *Peter Osnos' Platform*, a Substack newsletter. It is presented here in chapter form to better emphasize an essential point: Lyndon Johnson and Robert McNamara, because of their personalities and positions, were held responsible for a war they both knew could not be won in any conventional sense. The chapters describe how their relationship evolved, leading to a break that neither man ever publicly acknowledged—an unusual display of loyalty at so high a level of responsibility.

Their relationship with others in that period, especially John, Robert, and Jackie Kennedy, was also significant in ways that were profound but defy easy portrayals of animus or devotion.

This, then, is an interpretive history based very largely on the words of the protagonists, framed by an author using a journalist's approach to a subject, avoiding as much as possible a partisan prism.

LBJ and McNamara

The Vietnam Partnership Destined to Fail

Introduction

★ ★ ★

History is based on events interpreted by chroniclers, scholars, journalists, novelists, poets, and participants. But as Robert McNamara told his editors at an early discussion session, commentators tend to oversimplify history. "*History isn't that simple*," he said. "*It's messy.*"

The facts of America's engagement with Vietnam, Cambodia, and Laos in the 1960s and '70s are well known. By 1975 the United States had withdrawn support for its allies in the region, leaving Indochina in the hands of regimes that called themselves communist but were actually an amalgam of autocratic identities.

The American experience in Vietnam, known there always as the "American war," ended in 1973 when the last U.S. combat troops left the country. The war has been portrayed in scores of studies like the Pentagon Papers, as well as in innumerable books, documentaries, and movies. The net is always the same: Whatever good intentions led to the U.S. involvement in the civil war between North and South Vietnam, the end was a failure, a defeat, a debacle, or a tragedy, depending on who is describing the outcome.

There are many explanations for what happened, a result that for more than fifty years has shaped the nation's political, cultural, and social norms. When we now say "Vietnam," we are going beyond a war to summarize the consequences of that effort in lives, treasure, and our national sense of pride and patriotism.

David Halberstam framed forever those responsible as "the best and the brightest," the title of his epic 1972 book and his ironic shorthand for the men of public stature who collectively devised and drove a policy that was to prove untenable. They were unable to preserve one-half of Vietnam from the spread of Marxism-Leninism-Maoism in Asia in the midst of the Cold War with the Soviet Union and in the aftermath of the Chinese Revolution, all with the possibility of nuclear war hanging overhead.

This book is not meant to reconsider what is already known about Vietnam. It has a different objective: to describe as nearly as possible why the personalities and character of two men in particular were the central factors in the decision to escalate a commitment of fewer than 20,000 advisers in 1963 to a force of more than 536,000 American troops in 1968, when it was already clear to both of them that victory in the conventional sense was an impossible goal.

These men were President Lyndon Baines Johnson and his secretary of defense, Robert Strange McNamara

Once Johnson and McNamara were gone from office,

the conflict went on for another four years, with a casualty rate among U.S. forces climbing to 58,000 dead, hundreds of thousands of wounded, and colossal Vietnamese devastation. Johnson's successor, Richard Nixon, and his chief adviser, Henry Kissinger, redefined the U.S. objective as—in the parlance of realpolitik—"the decent interval" between the end of American involvement in the war and the now-presumed North Vietnamese triumph.

But it was Johnson and McNamara whose names and reputations were to be most closely connected to so profound a failure. They did not connive to produce policies. They were collaborators with others in devising them. But the depth, detail, and frequency of their contacts inevitably became a partnership of choices and, up to the point of their break, judgments.

Many others had important roles during the Vietnam era, including President John F. Kennedy and his brother Robert; McGeorge Bundy, Dean Rusk, and a cadre of White House and State Department officials; the Joint Chiefs of Staff, General William Westmoreland, and other military commanders; Ambassadors Henry Cabot Lodge, Maxwell Taylor, and Ellsworth Bunker; and Clark Clifford, a counselor to presidents from Harry S. Truman to Lyndon B. Johnson and McNamara's successor as secretary of defense as peace negotiations began in Paris.

There were no women among the policy makers to be held accountable, but there were two women who were part of the saga in their own way. The first was Jacqueline

Kennedy, not as first lady but for her influence as a widow on Johnson, McNamara, and her brother-in-law Robert. And second was Claudia "Lady Bird" Johnson, who more than anyone else monitored her husband's descent into despair over a battle he waged with public determination and private anguish. She watched how his extraordinary efforts on behalf of civil rights and social reform were upended emotionally by recognition of his confusion and frustration over Vietnam.

★ ★ ★ ★ ★

For more than ten years I worked with Robert McNamara on three books: his war memoir, *In Retrospect: The Lessons and Tragedy of Vietnam*; *Argument Without End: In Search of Answers to the Vietnam Tragedy*; and *Wilson's Ghost: Reducing the Risk of Conflict, Killing, and Catastrophe in the 21st Century*. I came to know him as his interlocutor, editor, publisher, and a person he could trust as he went through the process of coming to terms with what Vietnam had wrought to the country, his family, and the way so many Americans held him in contempt for his responsibility in what happened.

I did not know Lyndon Johnson personally, but because of the hundreds of hours of secret tapes made by him and now released, the extraordinary depth of Robert Caro's biographical portrait so far, and Lady Bird's amazing perceptiveness of his torment as recorded in her diaries, Johnson has been revealed in a way that it is fair to conclude no other American president has been.

From all the available material in the library of biographies, histories, and analyses of the period, the decades of my own involvement in the subject as a reporter and later as an editor, as well as access to the torrent of words in transcripts of my time with McNamara and the Johnson tapes, a picture of the men emerges that I intend to examine in the pages that follow, with this conclusion:

If John F. Kennedy had not been assassinated on November 22, 1963, and if Robert McNamara had been a man who was as politically astute as he was believed to be accomplished as a manager, and if Lyndon Johnson had been less a captive of insecurities eroding his judgment and spirit, then the misbegotten escalation in Vietnam might well have been avoided.

The United States of America was a superpower in those years in so many ways that the saga of Vietnam would seem to be inconceivable, except that it happened.

★ ★ ★ ★ ★

This book begins with the presidency of John F. Kennedy and continues year by year through the term of Lyndon B. Johnson.

The first chapter covers 1961-63, the Kennedy years, during which the Cold War with the Soviet Union was at its height, but the tense and perilous face-offs in Berlin and Cuba did not lead to the conflagrations that were feared. The movement for civil rights featured nonviolent protest, conveying a sense of dignified determination to defy racism, even as those resistant to racial integration often employed violent means themselves.

Overall, the mood in the country seemed to be lifted by the dynamic, glamorous presence of Kennedy, his family, and his cohort. The period has been romanticized and sentimentalized by its violent climax. There is resonance in what Daniel Patrick Moynihan said to his friend, the columnist Mary McGrory, after Kennedy was killed and she commented: "We'll never laugh again."

"We'll laugh again," Moynihan replied, "but we'll never be young again."

While the outcome of the Vietnam conflict is indisputable, the looming and unanswerable question is what John F. Kennedy would have done if he had lived. The record of the Kennedy years shows that the humiliation of the 1961 Bay of Pigs fiasco in his first year in office, when the young president concluded that he had been misled by the CIA and the military, followed in 1962 by the Cuban Missile Crisis, when Kennedy overruled those who favored a military solution, likely would have meant that he would adhere to his belief that the war in Vietnam was up to the Vietnamese to wage—and not to be the object of American intervention on a vast scale.

Historians now generally agree that Kennedy was killed before he had made a conclusive decision about whether the U.S. would be out of Vietnam by 1965. Decades after the fact, McNamara was certain that this would have been Kennedy's goal, but he never publicly went as far in his public statements as he did in sessions with his editors.

McNamara's selection as secretary of defense was itself not predictable. He had only recently been named president of the Ford Motor Company in the fall of 1960, and he did not know John Kennedy personally. When the president-elect offered him the job, McNamara said he was not qualified. But within days, the appointment was announced on the snowy steps of Kennedy's residence in Georgetown.

Like Kennedy, McNamara was young, just forty-four when he took the reins at the Pentagon. He had no particular political affiliation (at the time of his appointment he was a registered Republican), but his manner exuded competence and confidence without arrogance—though, ironically, arrogance would later be considered his defining personality trait.

McNamara was not from the establishment elite, in contrast to McGeorge Bundy, the new national security adviser. Though he had been to Harvard Business School for graduate study, he spent his college years at the University of California at Berkeley. But over time McNamara grew so close to the Kennedy family that he was asked to be at Andrews Air Force Base when the president's casket arrived from Dallas on the night of the assassination.

Chapter 2 covers the events of 1964 and the accession of Lyndon Johnson, who called himself "an accidental president." Once powerful as the Senate majority leader, Johnson as vice president had been degraded politically and personally to the extent that he had intended to remove himself from the Kennedy ticket in 1964.

Yet suddenly he had the position and the power that he had sought for so long. From all accounts, he was resolved to be elected for a term in his own right in 1964 and use the power of the presidency to pursue what he called the "Great Society"—government programs that would make America the nation of its unfulfilled founding principles. McNamara and most of JFK's senior leadership team made the transition to Johnson knowing that continuity was important after the shattering impact of Kennedy's death.

One of McNamara's strengths of character that had made him successful at Ford was understanding hierarchy and whose voice mattered most. So, as Johnson settled in, McNamara made himself valuable—even, in Johnson's terms, indispensable.

On Vietnam, with the benefit of hindsight, 1964 was the year Johnson kept all the issues unresolved as he ran for president. And McNamara, knowing how badly things were going on the war front, went along with Johnson's indecision, regardless of what he might have thought otherwise. Events in Vietnam—the successes of the Vietcong and the North Vietnamese combined with the political

INTRODUCTION

fracas in Saigon, where coups and juntas prevailed—were a distraction to be minimized at all costs during Johnson's 1964 presidential campaign against Senator Barry Goldwater, who was an all-out war hawk.

The Tonkin Gulf dustups in August 1964, in which there was a flareup of naval exchanges and bombing raids followed by a congressional resolution authorizing Johnson to go to war as he saw fit, did not move the president off his insistence on maintaining the "status quo" for U.S. involvement in the conflict during the campaign.

Johnson's landslide victory over Goldwater was a triumph of domestic politics and meant that the situation in Vietnam had to be confronted at last.

Chapter 3 moves on to the pivotal year of 1965, when the United States made a full commitment to the war in Vietnam, deploying combat forces and initiating a major bombing campaign. Between January and July, escalation proceeded apace, inextricably shifting the strategy from a war to be fought by the Vietnamese to the "American war." While a complete victory over Hanoi would have been the desired triumph, the formula that had held on the divided Korean peninsula, with "a free and independent South Vietnam," would likely have been acceptable as well.

Only days after Johnson's inaugural, McNamara and Bundy submitted a memo to the president captioned "Fork in the Road." The opening sentence was blunt: "Both of us are now pretty well convinced that our current policy can only lead to disastrous defeat." A month later, the Rolling

Thunder bombing campaign was underway, intended to stop North Vietnamese supplies to its Vietcong allies in the South and to bolster the South Vietnamese military morale. The bombing would continue with little letup until October 31, 1968.

On March 8, the 9th Marine Expeditionary Brigade arrived in Danang, the first deployment of a U.S. ground combat unit to Vietnam. In the months to follow, their mission was changed from base security to offensive operations.

All that spring and summer, there were meetings of national security officials and Pentagon leaders making plans and ultimately decisions to fundamentally alter the dynamic of the war, making it the "American war," to be conducted with the partnership of South Vietnamese troops who were never really respected by their U.S. counterparts.

What was in Lyndon Johnson's mind during those months seems contradictory and confusing. On February 11, Lady Bird recorded in her diary hearing the president say to his vice president, Hubert Humphrey, that he did not believe himself to be "qualified" to be commander-in-chief of the armed forces.

In late July, at Camp David, McNamara—now considered an advocate of escalation even though he was skeptical about the bombing strategy—was tasked by Johnson to debate Clark Clifford, a presidential senior adviser without portfolio, on the plan submitted by General William

INTRODUCTION

Westmoreland in Saigon for the deployment of 185,000 American troops by the end of the year.

McNamara argued in favor, Clifford against. Johnson's aide Jack Valenti kept notes.

Privately, McGeorge Bundy concluded years later for his unfinished memoir that Johnson had already agreed to move forward with the added forces. The debates, Bundy said, were more of a political exercise than a strategic one.

And what was in McNamara's mind?

McNamara had come to accept where the process was headed and was by instinct a supporter of the president's prerogative to decide. He, like other senior advisers, accepted the proposition that withdrawal would lead to communist domination of Southeast Asia. It was the height of the Cold War, only fifteen years after the People's Republic of China had intervened on behalf of communist North Korea during the Korean War, and so the concept of the U.S. giving up in Vietnam was inconceivable. It was also an era when national security thinking was centered on the "domino theory," which asserted that the fall of any one country to communism would lead to a communist takeover of neighboring countries. This was the view of many of the so called "Wise Men" of venerable former foreign officials and of former President Dwight Eisenhower, the World War II hero whose expertise was thought beyond challenge.

While a negotiated settlement might emerge, the North Vietnamese, it came to be believed, had to be persuaded that the United States would use whatever force was necessary to persuade them to concede. The U.S. military even considered the possibility of nuclear weapons.

Chapter 4 takes the story to 1966, the year of reckoning. A thirty-seven-day bombing pause, starting in December 1965 at McNamara's instigation, had not had any results that would suggest that negotiations with North Vietnam were possible.

The U.S. military was now deployed in force in Vietnam. McGeorge Bundy gave up his role at the National Security Council, recognizing that he no longer could work effectively with Johnson. He became president of the Ford Foundation and was never really held in judgment for his White House role. He was replaced by his deputy, Walt Rostow, who was a staunch advocate of waging all-out war.

The events of the year did not reverse the negative trends, despite the Johnson administration's persistence in releasing misleading reports that claimed the war was going well. As the difference between upbeat official assessments and field reporting by journalists took hold in the public, what was called the "credibility gap" arose, which over the years would harden into a general public skepticism toward government pronouncements.

LBJ's legislative strengths in securing passage of his Great Society programs on the domestic policy front were as formidable as his management of the war continued to be challenged by the enemy and on the home front.

INTRODUCTION

Senator William Fulbright, the chairman of the Senate Foreign Relations Committee, held nationally televised hearings that featured policy experts critical of the war. Questions began to be asked: How far could Johnson go in expanding the war? How should the administration handle the growing anti-war movement?

The conflict became known as "McNamara's war," and the secretary of defense said that he had no problem with that. But he continued to believe at some level that despite the massive American commitment, the military and political weaknesses of the South Vietnamese were likely to prevent anything like a conventional battlefield victory.

Chapter 5 recounts the events of 1967, when McNamara came to terms with the prospect of failure. He could no longer make the case that more troops would ever be enough. The possibility of a negotiated settlement was considered, and some forays were made without results. In April of that year, the Rev. Martin Luther King Jr. delivered a sermon at Riverside Church in New York opposing the war, complicating the relationship that he and others had developed with Johnson on civil rights.

By the end of the year, McNamara had decided to resign. His own relations with LBJ were now tense.

While the taped record is not clear, a complicating issue was McNamara's closeness to the Kennedy family. Robert Kennedy and Lyndon Johnson detested each other for a number of reasons, political and personal. McNamara was also close to Jackie Kennedy, a true friendship as distinct from Johnson's fawning efforts to reach out to her. And she was deeply opposed to the war.

Johnson devised the means to have McNamara appointed president of the World Bank, a move so deft that the secretary of defense could always maintain that he never really knew if he had been fired or if he had quit.

As chapter 6 shows, by 1968 Johnson was finished with McNamara, calling him a "screwball" in a call with a reporter. He named Clark Clifford as McNamara's successor, finally persuading the reluctant counselor to put his impeccable reputation to the test in policy. Clifford had the extraordinary ability to smooth talk in all situations, including dealing with Johnson's belief that Robert Kennedy, now in the Senate, was intent on driving him from office and restoring the Kennedy name to the presidency.

Clifford's own views on the war had evolved from his initial skepticism, and he was now considered a supporter of whatever was necessary. Upon taking office, however, Clifford quickly understood just how badly things were trending. His advice to Johnson soon became very much the same as McNamara's had been.

The word in Washington was that McNamara was at his wit's end, near a breakdown. When he was emotionally overcome at his retirement ceremony and unable to speak, that perception was widely accepted.

McNamara insisted that this was not the case. His tendency to weep when he was under certain forms of stress or

INTRODUCTION

after he had been drinking a bit was a behavioral tic that enabled his critics, ultimately, to mock his statements of regret about the war three decades later.

After setbacks in Vietnam, most notably the Tet offensive, and with Eugene McCarthy and Robert Kennedy announcing their candidacies for the Democratic presidential nomination, LBJ realized that he could not continue his reelection campaign.

And so, on March 31, he announced to a stunned nation that he would not run. Despite having committed himself to a search for peace, Johnson did not make any significant changes in strategy that might have led to negotiations—either in the bombing campaign or troop tactics. Violence soon convulsed America at home as well. On April 4, Martin Luther King was assassinated, followed by nationwide riots. And on June 5, Kennedy was shot; he died the next day.

After leaving the Pentagon, McNamara went on a vacation trip to Colorado with his wife before starting at the World Bank. Johnson was now a lame duck with a crushed morale. Their failed partnership was complete.

The war would go on. The devastation of Vietnam and the bombing of the North would wreak havoc, but not submission. The war would spread into Cambodia and, largely unnoticed, continue in Laos. A great many more American soldiers would be killed, wounded, or captured. The Pentagon Papers, initiated by McNamara, would reveal the scale of ignorance and duplicity that were so much a factor in the way the conflict unfolded on the battlefield and on American public attitudes.

Johnson's will was broken, and he died on January 22, 1973, the week his successor, Richard Nixon, was claiming that United States had achieved "peace with honor" in Vietnam, in the words of Henry Kissinger. The last American GIs and prisoners of war would leave the country in a matter of weeks.

One of the eternal debates in history is whether individuals shape events or whether it is the events that define the people involved in them.

The LBJ-McNamara relationship between 1963 and 1968 demonstrates how the personalities and character of these two men delivered an outcome neither of them actually wanted.

The tragedy was traceable to errors of judgment—choices in matters tactical, strategic, and practical.

But above all neither Johnson nor McNamara seemed to accept the moral implications of the conflict, that killing so many people because of a perceived need to defeat an ideology in a country they did not know or understand would defame them forever in history.

Johnson was destroyed by his failure—and by the consequences for his noble intentions on civil rights and poverty.

McNamara was doing his duty to the presidency as he saw it. But throughout his seven years as secretary of defense and for decades after, the way he carried himself—his slicked-back hair and his declaratory manner of speech—obscured the emotion beneath. And when it did show, it came across as self-pity.

They were not by nature evil men, but even though they knew and recognized that the mission in Vietnam encompassed evil, they were unable to end it. Robert McNamara did his best at explaining what had gone wrong. It would never be seen as enough.

Chapter One
The Kennedy Years

★ ★ ★

Secretary of Defense Robert McNamara was in a Pentagon budget meeting with senior military and civilian leaders about the upcoming budget and congressional debates at two p.m. on Friday, November 22, 1963.

McNamara's intention was to go to Hyannis Port a few days later, to brief President Kennedy on the results after the president returned from his trip to Texas.

"In the midst of a discussion," McNamara wrote in a draft chapter for his memoir *In Retrospect*, "my secretary reported a personal phone call..." in which he learned from Attorney General Robert Kennedy that the president had been shot.

In the transcripts of a recorded session in 1993 with his editors, this exchange followed:

Editor: How could you have gone on with your meeting?

McNamara: Well—well, in the first place he wasn't killed—the first point. Well, I stopped the meeting the moment I got the second call he was dead.

Editor: Yes, but even ...

McNamara: But in the first one ...

Editor: The president had been shot. You were the secretary of defense. How come you didn't go instantly ... I mean, what if this was the beginning of an international coup? ...

McNamara: Well, it didn't appear that way. In any case, the simple fact is that I didn't, the meeting did continue ...

Editor: But maybe you were in shock?

McNamara: No, no, definitely not that. Now what it was, we didn't think that it was serious, or we didn't think there was anything we could do about it other than go ahead with the meeting ...

In the book, after some consideration, McNamara wrote this about the meeting and the aftermath:

> My secretary informed me of an urgent, personal telephone call. I left the conference room and took it alone in my office. It was Bobby Kennedy, even more lonely and distant than usual. He told me simply and quietly that the president had been shot.
>
> I was stunned. Slowly, I walked back to the conference room and, barely controlling my voice, reported the news to the group. Strange as it may sound, we did not disperse: we were in such shock that we simply did not know what to do. So, as best we could, we resumed our deliberations.

A second call from Bobby came about forty-five minutes later. The president was dead. Our meeting was immediately adjourned amid tears and stunned silence.

McNamara gathered the Joint Chiefs of Staff and ordered U.S. military forces worldwide to be placed on alert. When the attorney general called again, it was to ask McNamara and Maxwell Taylor, the president's top military adviser, to accompany him to Andrews Air Force Base to meet the returning casket.

> Shortly after we arrived at Andrews, the blue and white presidential jet slowly taxied up to the terminal, its landing lights still on. Bobby turned and asked me to board the plane with him. It so clearly seemed a moment of intimacy and privacy for a family in sorrow that I refused ...
>
> The Kennedys and I had started as strangers but had grown very close. Unlike many subsequent administrations, they drew in some of their associates, transforming them from colleagues to friends. We could laugh with one another. And we could cry with one another. It had been that way with me, and that made the president's death even more devastating.

Bobby now called to say that Jackie Kennedy wanted McNamara to join her at Bethesda Naval Hospital while she awaited the outcome of the autopsy.

> I drove immediately to the hospital and sat with Jackie, Bobby, and other family members and friends. In the early morning hours, we accompanied the president's body back to the White House, where the casket was placed in the elegant East Room, draped by the flag he had served and loved and lit softly by candles.

In the transcript, the closeness of McNamara to the Kennedys, and especially to Bobby, is especially vivid.

Editor: Under those circumstances would you be the person that they would turn to?

McNamara: Well, among the cabinet ... But you see [Bobby] called me to go out [to Andrews] with him. And then, after we got there, he wanted me to board the plane. It was a very poignant moment. Here's Johnson [also on Air Force One after being sworn in], and he didn't give a damn about Johnson. I wasn't there because of Johnson. Bobby just wanted me to go up with him, up the stairs and meet Jackie ...

Editor: I mean Dean Rusk wasn't there ...

McNamara: Oh, hell no.

Editor: Mac Bundy wasn't there.

McNamara: No, no.

Editor: So that, in today's jargon, it would be correct to say that you had bonded ...

McNamara: Oh, absolutely. No question about it ... We bonded because we had shared values, number one, and [with Bobby] a shared sense of loyalty to the president. Bobby knew that I was loyal to the president. And he also, in a sense, knew that I was loyal to him.

★ ★ ★ ★ ★

November 22, 1963, was the day that everything changed.

William Manchester's intricately detailed account of that day, *The Death of a President*, provides names, places, and reactions to the news as word spread of John F. Kennedy's assassination. Most people, wrote Manchester, simply could not believe what had happened, even after his death was confirmed at Parkland Hospital in Dallas.

The tenor of the country was suddenly transformed. The indelible images of that weekend were of the widow and children attending the burial at Arlington; John Jr. saluting his father's casket; and Lee Harvey Oswald being shot to death in a Dallas police station by Jack Ruby. Those moments were especially powerful because they were shown live on television. Tens of millions of Americans shared the drama and for all, very young to very old, they were never to be forgotten. Quite literally for the first time, every American could be present at the same historical moments.

Something else was happening that weekend. The presidency was being transferred from the New Frontier of John F. Kennedy and his cohort to Lyndon Johnson, who as an American political figure was from an entirely different culture, not by generation but in every other way. As a personality, Kennedy was elegant and cool. Johnson was intense and physically awesome. He came from the hardscrabble Texas hinterland, and his political trajectory was rough and tumble, whereas Kennedy's was, at least as seen by the public at that time, smooth.

When LBJ ascended to majority leader of the Democrats in the U.S. Senate, he was brilliant in the handling of power; his biographer Robert Caro's volume on those years is titled *Master of the Senate*. In 1960, his bid for his party's presidential nomination was clumsy and ended at the Democratic National Convention, where in a fraught process leaving bruises on all involved he was named to the ticket as vice president, ostensibly to make Kennedy more palatable to voters in the southern states.

Biographers' accounts of Johnson as vice president describe a time of indignity and mishap. Kennedy himself did not turn on Johnson but used him sparingly on any matters of consequence. The president's brother Bobby, on the other hand, pursued a personal animus for LBJ, and the overall sense in Washington was that Johnson had been humiliated.

After Kennedy's day in Dallas, he had been scheduled to fly to the LBJ Ranch for an evening with Johnson and

Lady Bird. All the preparations for the presidential stopover were complete.

As the historian Max Holland writes in the introduction to his book *Presidential Recordings: Lyndon B. Johnson*:

> Lyndon Johnson rarely got to spend an extended amount of time with the President under such casual circumstances and intended to use the occasion to discuss his most pressing concern: his place on the November 3 ballot, less than a year away. Within political circles and the media, rumors abounded that Johnson would be unceremoniously dumped from the Democratic ticket ...
>
> The Vice President's pride was deeply wounded, for he had taken great pains to be loyal to the administration and did not deserve to be treated this way. Such rumors did not arise on their own in Washington; someone credible in the administration had to be generating speculation or doing something. Consequently, the Vice President intended to use the evening of November 22 to deliver a stunning message of his own.
>
> Lyndon Johnson did not want to be on the Democratic ticket in 1964.

This revelation also appears in Kenneth W. Thompson's book, *The Johnson Presidency: Twenty Intimate Perspectives of Lyndon B. Johnson*. Another version has Johnson stepping down to become president of his alma mater, the Southwest Texas State Teachers College in San Marcos.

Whatever the case may have been, by the evening of November 22, 1963, the world had changed. Lyndon Johnson was now the president of the United States and had flown to Washington to assume the office and its responsibilities.

★ ★ ★ ★ ★

The victory of the Kennedy-Johnson ticket in 1960 over Richard Nixon and Henry Cabot Lodge Jr. (who would later serve as the U.S. ambassador in South Vietnam for Kennedy) was by a narrow margin. The role played by Mayor Richard J. Daley of Chicago in securing a victory in Illinois that had sealed the win for Kennedy was regarded with some suspicion—a reflection of the fact that when it came to political goals, the Kennedy family and their operatives knew hardball.

But as the appointments to the White House staff and the cabinet went forward leading up to the January inauguration, the choices were considered notable for their distinction and personal dignity. Dean Rusk, a former Rhodes Scholar who was president of the Rockefeller Foundation in New York, was named secretary of state.

Douglas Dillon, a patrician investment banker, was the new secretary of the treasury, and McGeorge Bundy, who had been named Dean of the Faculty of Arts and Sciences at Harvard at age thirty-four, was to be the national security adviser.

Robert S. McNamara, the incoming secretary of defense, had served under General Curtis LeMay as one of the men who planned bombing raids over Japan, which were in time responsible for hundreds of thousands of Japanese dead, the majority of whom were civilians.

In Errol Morris's Oscar-winning documentary, *The Fog of War,* McNamara quoted LeMay as saying later, "If we'd lost the war, we'd all have been prosecuted as war criminals." McNamara then observed, "And I think he's right. He, and I'd say I, were behaving as war criminals. LeMay recognized that what he was doing would be thought immoral if his side had lost. But what makes it immoral if you lose and not immoral if you win?"

LeMay's bombast was instinctive. As a bomb spotter in World War II, McNamara had been a technocrat.

In the immediate postwar years, any personal reflections of McNamara's role in the war were doubtless submerged beneath the surface as he focused on his career and the family he started with his beloved wife, Marg. After his military service he had joined the Ford Motor Company as one of the "Whiz Kids," with a mandate to modernize the automaker, rising to the position of president of the company in late October 1960. Then, on December 8, only weeks later, McNamara was approached by Sargent Shriver, JFK's brother-in-law, who said he was authorized to offer him the position of secretary of defense.

"This is absurd!" McNamara replied. "I'm not qualified."

Two people had recommended McNamara to the president-elect: John Kenneth Galbraith, the famed Harvard economics professor, and Robert Lovett, a former secretary of defense and a senior figure in the group of former officials who came to be known as "The Wise Men" because of their stature and national security experience. Significantly, these men had all been shaped by their experiences in World War II and the Soviet-American power clash, with the potential of a nuclear war that in the 1950s was a permanent threat. Also, there had been a communist takeover in China, followed by the war in Korea.

When McNamara told Kennedy that he was not qualified by experience to be secretary of defense, Kennedy replied, "Who is?" There were no schools for defense secretaries, Kennedy observed, "and no schools for presidents either."

For all his management success at Ford and reputation for effectiveness, McNamara had this private worry:

What do I know about the application of force and what do I know about the strategy required to defend the West against what was a generally accepted threat ... [and] the force structure necessary to effectively counter the threat?

Personal doubt as a senior government official—

a recognition of limitations—then or thereafter were not meant to be worthy of serious consideration in policy debates. Once named, a secretary of defense was assumed to be qualified.

When McNamara agreed to take the job, Kennedy immediately announced it, and the televised images were of these two vigorous men in their early forties, showing none of whatever qualms they may have had about the jobs they were assuming.

McNamara's primary challenge, as it had been at Ford, was to oversee the management and operations of a vast infrastructure that needed to be modernized. To achieve this, McNamara had insisted as a condition of taking the job that Kennedy let him make all appointments on his own.

This led to a particular disagreement over the post of secretary of the navy. McNamara read an article in *The New York Times* that reported that Franklin D. Roosevelt Jr. was to be named to the post.

In our editorial session transcript, McNamara recalled:

I didn't pay attention. I didn't realize that was [Kennedy's] desire, and somebody leaked it and it was a done deal. I go along, couple of weeks, and I'm appointing people, and the president's approving them all, and he says, "Bob, you are making wonderful progress, but you haven't recommended anyone for secretary of the navy."

I said, "Mr. President, I just can't find the right person."

"Well," he said, "have you thought of Franklin Roosevelt?"

"Well," I said, "Hell, he's a drunken womanizer."
And he said, "Well, have you met him?"
And I said, "No, I haven't."
"Well, he said, "don't you think you ought to meet him before you make a decision?"
I said, "Sure, I'll be happy to. Where in the hell is this guy?"
"Well, he's a Fiat dealer."
So, I got the Yellow Pages out, looked down. I found the Fiat place in Washington, got him there and I ...

I don't know that they ever met. Ultimately, Roosevelt was named undersecretary of commerce. McNamara's choice for the navy position was John Connally of Texas, who had been LBJ's campaign manager at the Democratic convention, which meant that Kennedy was well aware of him and might well have been suspicious of his loyalty. Connally got the job and served until he resigned to run for governor in 1962. (And in 1963, he was in Kennedy's car on the day the president was killed. He was wounded himself and nearly died.) Connally later switched parties became a powerful figure in the Republican Party, and he ran, unsuccessfully, in 1980 for its presidential nomination.

McNamara recalled:

I was right on Franklin Roosevelt, and I was right on Connally. Connally was one of the loyalest people in town for Kennedy ... [The president] knew he had made a deal with me. He knew he was going to lose a secretary of defense if he didn't go along this way, and he would have ...

And that's one of the things that bonded us. You know, I loved the guy. But I had certain standards. I had certain requirements. He understood them and he knew God-damned well I was going to do them.

McNamara was using this episode as a way of framing his relationship with JFK, and the savvy management of political issues as they arose, working around the problem together rather than turning stubbornness into a damaging confrontation.

In *The Fog of War,* Errol Morris asked McNamara how far he would go in challenging presidential authority, the role he might have played as Vietnam moved to the center of LBJ's years in office, and whether he might have held his ground when there were policy issues on which he and the president disagreed. This answer, repeated in various formats over the ensuing years, would be McNamara's explanation: He was an appointed adviser to the person with the election mandate to decide.

> Morris: To what extent did you feel that you were the author of stuff, or that you were an instrument of things outside your control?
>
> McNamara: Well, I don't think I felt either. I just felt that I was serving at the request of the president, who had been elected by the American people. And it was my responsibility to try to help him carry out the office as he believed was in the interest of our people.

When it came to Vietnam, this was not a challenge for McNamara in dealing with Kennedy, as it was later to become with Johnson. In October 1963, Kennedy and McNamara were making contingency plans to start withdrawing the 16,000 military advisers the U.S. then had in Vietnam. It was Kennedy's strong opinion that the war was South Vietnam's to fight and win—and should not be America's responsibility.

Having just returned from a survey trip to Vietnam that fall, McNamara knew the situation there—militarily across the country and in Saigon, where the political scene was increasingly chaotic and getting worse. That reality then and thereafter was what McNamara knew to be the case—but was not what he would say in his many public opportunities to do so.

And then Kennedy was assassinated. The signoff on an American withdrawal was tabled. What JFK would have done in 1964, 1965, and beyond will never be known.

★ ★ ★ ★ ★

The thousand days of the Kennedy presidency were, on the whole, a period in which the American domestic situation was, by historic standards, relatively stable. The civil rights confrontations in the South were increasing—as when Kennedy had to call out the National Guard to accompany James Meredith in 1962 as he sought to become the first Black student at the University of Mississippi.

Congressional action was stymied by the nature of the Democratic majority, which consisted of labor activists and liberals in the North and segregationists in the South, including some of the most powerful politicians of that era. The Republican Party was beginning its long-term evolution from Eastern establishment figures like Governor Nelson Rockefeller of New York to conservatives like Senator Barry Goldwater of Arizona, who was to become the party's firebrand pro-war candidate for president in 1964.

In foreign policy, to the extent that there was a bipartisan position, it was based on developments in the Cold War with the Soviet Union. The question was not whether to accept the Soviets as a great power and recognize Mao Zedong's Communist China, but how far to go in taking them on for global influence and power. In the McCarthy period of the early 1950s, anyone who could be tainted with a hint of subversive activity or thoughts was persecuted, blacklisted, or jailed—and that included leading State Department experts on China.

The Korean War, which had ended in a stalemate in 1953, had resulted in an unequivocal and potentially dangerous U.S. role on the peninsula. And in Europe, a divided Berlin was the proverbial flashpoint for war. When the Berlin Wall was erected in the summer of 1961, Soviet intentions were deemed hostile to the extreme. The possibility of an all-out nuclear exchange reached its apogee the following year, when Soviet missiles were placed in Cuba, putting much of the United States within range.

Two episodes in particular would shape Kennedy's approach to dealing with Vietnam, which at the time seemed a distant and not especially urgent problem. An International Agreement on the Neutrality of Laos at the end of a sixteen-nation conference in Geneva in 1962 essentially removed one of the Indochina states from the center of Cold War disputes. Settling the Laos issue was in itself not terribly significant, but it did mean that under the right circumstances, a negotiated outcome to conflict in Asia was possible.

But more prominent in Kennedy's mind was the Bay of Pigs debacle. In April 1961, a group of Cuban exiles with CIA backing and Pentagon support were demolished just days after their invasion of the island, with the goal of wresting it away from Fidel Castro's revolutionary government. This was a searing early lesson in failure for JFK, though it received short narrative shrift in the early pages of McNamara's memoirs and in our discussions.

The Eisenhower administration had authorized the CIA to organize a brigade of 1,400 Cuban exiles as an invasion force to overthrow Castro, who had seized power in 1959 and had since become an avowed supporter of Soviet-style communism. The new Kennedy administration had allowed preparations for the invasion to carry on. "For three months after President Kennedy's inauguration," McNamara writes in *In Retrospect*, "we felt as though we were on a roll. But only a few days after he presented the defense blueprint to Congress, we faced a decision that showed our judgment—and our luck—had severe limitations."

Kennedy, McNamara writes, gathered about twenty of his advisers to a State Department meeting to make a final decision on whether to proceed. Only one person, Senator William Fulbright, dissented "vigorously." The Joint Chiefs of Staff endorsed the plan, as did Secretary of State Dean Rusk and McGeorge Bundy. McNamara concurred as well, "although not enthusiastic."

The invasion launched on April 17, 1961, and McNamara quotes a historian who called it "a perfect failure." It ended in days, with the invaders killed, wounded, or captured. Watching JFK on national television taking "full responsibility" was a "bitter lesson" for McNamara:

> I had entered the Pentagon with a limited grasp of military affairs and even less grasp of covert operations. This lack of understanding, coupled with my preoccupation with other matters and my deference to the CIA on what I considered an agency operation, led me to accept the plan uncritically. I had listened to the briefings ... I had even passed along to the president, without comment, an ambiguous assessment by the Joint Chiefs that the invasion would probably contribute to Castro's overthrow even if it did not succeed right away. The truth

is I did not understand the plan very well and did not know the facts. I had let myself become a passive bystander.

When McNamara met with Kennedy and offered to take his measure of the blame, the president said that this was unnecessary. "I did not have to do what of all you recommended," Kennedy said. "I did it. I am responsible and I will not try to put part of the blame on you, or Eisenhower, or anyone else."

McNamara adds: "I admired him for that, and the incident brought us closer. I made up my mind not to let him down again."

McGeorge Bundy never completed his version of a memoir, although he worked with the historian Gordon M. Goldstein in preparing one. Goldstein published his own book, *Lessons in Disaster: McGeorge Bundy and the Path to War in Vietnam,* based on their discussions and on those parts of the book Bundy had drafted before he died.

Lesson one for Bundy, Goldstein writes, grew out of the Bay of Pigs experience. That lesson was: "Counselors Advise but Presidents Decide."

This straightforward summary explains why, after the Bay of Pigs and as American escalation in Vietnam grew through the Johnson years, the president sought advice but only he, LBJ, could make the final decisions. And Johnson's decisions were always made with politics uppermost in his mind. Beneath the surface, and not visible to others, were his doubts and confusions about the choices he was making.

★ ★ ★ ★ ★

The account provided by McNamara and many other participants and writers about the Cuban Missile Crisis in October 1962 shows how Kennedy was surrounded by senior officials and advisers recommending military intervention in Cuba to force the Soviets to remove the weapons it had placed there. Instead, he chose to use a naval blockade and some secret bargaining over U.S. missiles in Turkey to end the confrontation.

On the evening of October 15, McGeorge Bundy was hosting a dinner party that was interrupted by a call from Ray Cline, the deputy director of the CIA, who said that reconnaissance photography had confirmed that the Soviet Union was deploying medium-range nuclear missiles in Cuba.

Bundy returned to the dinner party without informing the president.

He later explained to Kennedy, "I decided that a quiet evening and a night of sleep were the best preparation you could have in light of what would face you in the next days."

At eight o'clock the next morning, with Kennedy still in his pajamas, sitting in bed reading the newspapers, Bundy informed him of the crisis.

Over the next thirteen days, Kennedy convened multiple sessions of advisers, designated the Executive Committee of the National Security Council, or "ExComm," to consider options for having the missiles removed. Among this group were the Soviet experts Charles (Chip) Bohlen,

George F. Kennan, and Llewellyn Thompson, whose collective experience with the Kremlin provided a level of insight that was especially valuable.

To highlight the intensity of the moment, McNamara told us in our editorial sessions that he never went home during the entire period. He slept at the Pentagon for the next twelve nights.

It wasn't that I felt the military wouldn't pursue the instructions we laid down, not at all ... It was that this was a very delicate communications problem between Kennedy and Khrushchev, and we didn't want a war and we wanted to get the goddamned missiles. How do you get the missiles out without a war? We put in the quarantine.

The deliberations that led to the outcome have been dissected and analyzed in any number of books and studies.

In Retrospect has this account:

> By Saturday, October 27, 1962—the height of the crisis—the majority of the president's military and civilian advisers were prepared to recommend that if Khrushchev did not remove the Soviet missiles from Cuba (which he agreed to the following day) the United States should attack the island. But Kennedy repeatedly made the point that Saturday—both in Executive Committee sessions and later, in a small meeting with Bobby, Dean, Mac, and me—that the

United States must make every effort to avoid the risk of an unpredictable war. He appeared willing, if necessary, to trade the obsolete American Jupiter missiles in Turkey for the Soviet missiles in Cuba in order to avert the risk. He knew such an action was strongly opposed by the Turks, by NATO, and by most senior U.S. State and Defense Department officials. But he was prepared to take that stand to keep us out of war.

Ultimately, the crisis ended with the blockade and secret agreement about the missiles in Turkey but remains the closest that the United States came to a confrontation with the Soviet Union over nuclear weapons. McNamara's view of the episode was framed around Kennedy's rejection of the advice of his Joint Chiefs to use force in Cuba. In our discussion, he said:

Had we invaded that island, as a majority of Kennedy's military and civilian advisers were recommending ... and they were recommending it be done three or four days later—attack and later invasion—those damn warheads would have been used, without any question.

Kennedy's position was:

He didn't believe that a president and I didn't believe a secretary of defense should expose our nation to even a small risk of a catastrophe. That's why I don't think he would have moved in Cuba.

As 1963 unfolded, the Saigon government of Ngo Dinh Diem and his brother Ngo Dinh Nhu had become increasingly fierce in its crackdown on the Buddhists who were critical of the Catholic-led regime. Diem held the leadership position with Nhu at his shoulder. The view in Washington was, as it so often was in similar circumstances, "He's a son of a bitch, but he's our son of a bitch." The view had been to do everything possible to support Diem. On June 11, Thich Quang Duc, a revered elder among the Buddhist monks, immolated himself in protest of the repression of the Buddhists, which Malcolm Browne of the Associated Press captured in a photograph that symbolized the scale of what was happening.

Restraining repression became a focal point of U.S. policy, along with a growing awareness of the successes in the countryside of the communist Vietcong guerrillas. How much pressure could be applied on Diem and Nhu? And there was a sense that some generals in the Armed Forces of the Republic of Vietnam (ARVN) were moving toward a coup. The U.S. ambassador in Saigon, Frederick Nolting, got along well with Diem, but his deputy, William Trueheart, took a much harder line with the South Vietnamese president when Nolting left Vietnam for six weeks at a moment of serious tension. Trueheart sided with those who wanted to oust Diem, whereas Nolting wanted to continue working with him. According to his son Charles Trueheart's book *Diplomats at War: Friendship and Betrayal on the Brink of the Vietnam Conflict*, Nolting on his return was furious.

In Washington, officials increasingly shared the sense that Diem and Nhu were unwilling and unable to change their attitudes and actions. The more the crackdown against Buddhists went forward—and the less it seemed that U.S. influence was working—the clearer it became that something had to be done.

By now it was high summer, and the principal decision makers were away from Washington. Kennedy was in Hyannis Port. McNamara and Marg were in the Grand Tetons. Rusk, Bundy, and CIA Director John McCone were all away as well.

On August 24, McNamara writes, "several of the officials we left behind saw an opportunity to move against the Diem regime. Before the day was out, the United States had set in motion a military coup, which I believe was one of the truly pivotal decisions concerning Vietnam made during the Kennedy and Johnson administrations."

McNamara identifies Roger Hilsman, the assistant secretary of state for Far Eastern affairs, as the prime mover of this effort: "Hilsman was a smart, abrasive, talk-ative West Point graduate ... He and his associates believed we could not win with Diem and, therefore Diem should be removed." Hilsman then drafted a cable to Henry Cabot Lodge Jr., who had just arrived in Saigon to replace Nolting as the new ambassador. The cable said:

It is now clear that whether the military proposed martial law or whether Nhu tricked them into it, Nhu took advantage of its imposition to smash pagodas ... Also clear that Nhu has maneuvered himself into commanding position.

U.S. Government cannot tolerate situation in which power lies in Nhu's hands. Diem must be given chance to rid himself of Nhu and his coterie and replace them with best military and political personalities available.

If, in spite of all your efforts, Diem remains obdurate and refuses, then we must face the possibility that Diem himself cannot be preserved.

As the draft cable ricocheted through the vacationing officials it was finally sent to Kennedy with assurances that it had been approved by the senior cabinet members, but because of the dispersal of the participants, this was more than had actually happened. Reluctantly, Kennedy said it was okay to transmit.

Only then was the cable shared with General Maxwell Taylor, the president's military adviser, a World War II hero "and the wisest uniformed geopolitician and security adviser I ever met," according to McNamara. Taylor had been appointed to that role because Kennedy knew that the Joint Chiefs of Staff as a group had been wrong in the Bay of Pigs and in the missile crisis, and while he trusted McNamara and Bundy, he did not trust the generals.

Taylor was shocked that the cable had already been sent. He called what the anti-Diem faction in Washington had done "an egregious end run" while high-ranking officials were away.

Cables and memoranda were the primary means of group communications in Washington and with Saigon. In meetings, differing views were shared and heard by all. But written communications increased the risks of misunderstanding—who wrote them, who received them and who did not, who read them and who did not. In our internet age, we encounter the same sort of problem—think of a mistyped "reply all," for example. The possibility that Diem could be removed was now in bureaucratic play. And the record indicates that Kennedy was equivocal in how own judgment on the situation—to his later chagrin.

There is no doubt that in the months of September and October the possibility of a military coup increased. But what happened on November 1 was not anticipated, at least by Kennedy. After Diem and Nhu had agreed to surrender, they were placed in an armored personnel carrier and murdered, with grisly photos of their bodies published worldwide.

Kennedy was appalled.

On Monday, November 4, he dictated this memo: "Over the weekend, the coup in Saigon took place, culminated three months of conversations about a coup, conversations which divided the government here and in Saigon. Opposed to a coup was General Taylor, the attorney general, Secretary McNamara ... In favor of the coup was State, led by Averell Harriman, George Ball, Roger Hilsman ... I feel that we must bear a good deal of responsibility for it beginning with our cable of early August in which we suggested the coup. In my judgment that wire was badly drafted, it should never have been sent on a Saturday."

(Kennedy did not mention Secretary of State Dean Rusk in this dictation, which over the years to come would show that Rusk never was as much of a confidant or influence on JFK and later Lyndon Johnson, as might be expected of a secretary of state. But he stayed in office until the end of Johnson's term.)

"I was shocked by the death of Diem and Nhu," Kennedy continued, adding that Diem "was an extraordinary character and while he became increasingly difficult in the last months, nevertheless over a ten-year period he held his country together to maintain its independence under very adverse conditions. The way he was killed made it particularly abhorrent. The question now, whether the generals can stay together and build a stable government ... "

They could not.

And so, on November 22, 1963, the political situation in Saigon was a mess and despite some professed claims of progress around the country, the downward trajectory was continuing. Kennedy's advisers were addled and squabbling over who did what to whom in fomenting the coup.

McNamara, in his book discussion with his editors, made the case—stronger than he would do elsewhere—that Kennedy would have proceeded with his planned withdrawal of U.S. forces in 1964 and 1965.

He would have, particularly, I think, recognized that the conditions we had laid down, specifically that he had stated categorically a few days before—i.e., it was a South Vietnamese war; it could only be won by them; and to do that they needed a sound political base—were not being met.

Therefore, whatever the costs of withdrawing—and, as I say, I think he would have thought they were greater than, with hindsight, we know them to have been—I say he would have accepted the domino theory back then ... He would have accepted that cost, because he knew that the conditions necessary to avoid it weren't there and couldn't be met and in an attempt to meet them, we would spill our blood, and he wasn't about to do that ...

This was also the conclusion of Clark Clifford, who knew Kennedy well and was later to be Johnson's secretary of defense. In an interview with his editors for his memoir *Counsel to the President,* Clifford said that JFK was firmly set against deploying ground troops to Vietnam. "In judging matters of this kind [Kennedy] was a real cold fish," Clifford said. "He could be totally objective ... under the façade of charm and attractiveness ... He was cold, calculating and penetrating." Clifford said that he could imagine

Kennedy concluding in so many words, "I'm not willing to take the chance. I don't like what I see ahead. I'm suspicious of the people who are involved. I just don't think I ought to accept the representations of the military with full faith and credit extended ... I'm just going to get more deeply involved in what is a stinking mess."

Nonetheless, the Kennedy presidency was unquestionably dominated by the belief—and reality—of Soviet and related communist threats in Europe and Asia. Kennedy's responses to those reflected an instinct, shared on the whole with McNamara, to deflect confrontations rather than meet them directly with force. His terrible experience with the Bay of Pigs, events around the building of the Berlin Wall in 1961, the Geneva conference in 1962 that ended with the neutralization of Laos, and the Cuban missile crisis demonstrated a strategy to avoid catastrophic outcomes.

McNamara believed that Kennedy had concluded that the pretext for the continuing war in Vietnam—to head off Soviet influence and Chinese participation in Asia, as had happened in Korea a decade earlier—was not worth the cost it would entail. In ways expressed by the Soviet expert George F. Kennan and politicians like Senator Fulbright (and by McNamara in the 1990s), exaggerating Soviet power and the overall communist threat was, in many ways, as bad and certainly as perilous as underestimating it.

As for Vietnam, McNamara said years later, Kennedy

and his advisers, for all their pizazz, were ignorant in almost every way possible about Southeast Asia, its languages, its history, its culture—and moreover, in a global battle with communism, Vietnam "was a tiny blip on the radar." But because "we screwed up," he said bluntly, the blip would eventually overwhelm so much else.

In discussing the Kennedy presidency, McNamara's editors returned again and again to the matter of what Kennedy would have done in Vietnam had he lived. Most historians tend to believe that Kennedy would have had to reverse the withdrawal of U.S. advisers, but this was not what McNamara believed.

Why would he make so firm a statement to the editors when he refused to make it publicly?

I'm doing it here for only one reason. Because if I think as I do—that he would have gotten out, then it is incumbent upon me to explain why those of us who worked with him, including Johnson, didn't get out ... I don't raise it because I'm not trying to ... vindicate Kennedy or admire him or support him or whatever.

I raise it only because the burden of proof is on those of us who stayed ... why the hell ...

Kennedy had all the members of his cabinet and the National Security Council read Barbara Tuchman's book *The Guns of August* about the origins of World War I. She reports one former German chancellor asking another, "How did it happen?"

The other replies, "I wish I knew." In other words, they bungled into war.

"I don't ever want to be in that position," Kennedy said. "We are not going to bungle into war."

Chapter Two
The Accidental President

★ ★ ★

THE FIRST DAYS OF LYNDON JOHNSON'S PRESIDENCY were a mass of confusion, grief, abrupt realignments in position and prospects, and an immediate cascade of urgent issues and decisions that had to be made.

The LBJ tapes of those days show a president managing what were immediate challenges, including the creation of what became the Warren Commission after Chief Justice Earl Warren was persuaded to investigate the assassination and deal with conspiracy theories that to this day have never been completely resolved. What to say in his first address to a joint session of Congress was, not surprisingly, extremely sensitive, and Johnson relied on Ted Sorensen, Kennedy's speechwriter, to get it right. And congressional action on the budget and taxes were a fixation for Johnson, who was doubtless relieved to be back in areas where he had experience rather than having to deal with the unprecedented aftermath of the martyrdom of a young president.

A great deal has been written about Johnson's relationship with the Kennedy family, especially Jackie and Bobby as they were always called, including by Johnson. Every conversation with the new widow in those days, and thereafter, was loving to the point of unctuousness, and she would respond with what sounded like purring. Altogether different was LBJ's loathing of the attorney general and Bobby's similar contempt for Johnson.

Johnson considered Bobby a political rival of major potential. For his part, Bobby, who so disliked LBJ he had tried to keep him off the 1960 ticket, considered the new president a usurper. The antagonism was beyond mediation.

William Manchester's book *The Death of a President* captures every iota of real and perceived slights in the early weeks of the transition. Johnson's combination of awe, envy, and suspicion of the Kennedys was a profoundly personal matter embedded in his character.

In time, the evolution of Bobby as heir to his brother's political mantle and Jackie, who became, privately, a passionate opponent of the Vietnam war, would be strands in the unraveling of Johnson's own judgment about the conflict. Because of McNamara's closeness to the Kennedy family, this was an aspect of his dealings with LBJ that was especially hard to parse.

McNamara was an unusually loyal person and in that, he was sincere—in this case to three people whose relationships defied explicable boundaries.

For example, in August 1964, at the start of what became known as the Tonkin Gulf incidents—a major turning point in the direct battle with North Vietnam—a critical meeting took place in the White House on the morning of August 2. McNamara told his editors that the record of the sessions reveals that he was not in attendance, only arriving later in the day.

Where the hell was I? I was at Newport with Jackie. She was at her mother's house, had stayed overnight. Marg was traveling and I went up and stayed overnight Saturday night with Jackie.

The point of the anecdote was that McNamara did not consider himself responsible, at least initially, for decisions about the Tonkin Gulf episode. In 1993, with Jackie alive at the time, he said, "*I was, and am close to Jackie. I'm very fond of her.*" This explanation for his absence from the meeting was omitted in his memoir.

Vietnam was very much on the crowded agenda in late 1963 and 1964, and Johnson held multiple meetings with the national security leadership, reflecting the reality that the situation in the country after the ouster of Diem and Nhu had only gotten worse.

Johnson decided to send McNamara to Vietnam again to assess the situation. Upon his return to Washington on December 21, McNamara publicly said, as quoted in *In Retrospect* with words he added to the statement: "'We observed the results of a very substantial increase in Vietcong activity' (true); but I then added, 'We reviewed the plans of the South Vietnamese and we have every reason to believe they will be successful' (an overstatement at best)."

He continues, "I was far more forthright—and gloomy—in my report to the president. 'The situation is very disturbing,' I told him, predicting that 'current trends, unless reversed in the next 2-3 months, will lead to neutralization at best or more likely to a Communist-controlled state.'"

In the memoir, McNamara raises, without answering, the question that was central to the reputation he developed for dissembling in his public appraisals of the war: "It is a profound, enduring, and universal ethical and moral dilemma: how, in times of war and crisis, can senior government officials be completely frank to their own people without giving aid and comfort to the enemy?"

And there is the essence of what would bedevil the Johnson administration going forward; consistently misleading the American public was a blunder with consequences then and to this day, well into the twenty-first century.

Vietnam and every other foreign policy issue at the height of the Cold War were subordinate, however, to Johnson's singular priority, winning the presidential election in November 1964. If elected in his own right, he could stop deriding himself as the "accidental president."

McNamara sparred with his editors over whether Johnson put off decisions on Vietnam solely for political reasons. The underlying problem, he insisted, was that there was no consensus among the military or among the president's advisers on what should be done. The solution was to adopt wording like "Hard as it may be to believe ... LBJ was not just making a political choice."

Nothing in LBJ's character, especially after the humiliation of the years as vice president, could possibly be more important to him than restoring his self-confidence as a politician and as a man with power and the capacity to use it.

The events of 1964 would be many but the record shows that nothing would be allowed to diminish Johnson's public stance in opposition to widening the Vietnam war, especially after the Republicans nominated Barry Goldwater, who was fierce in his assertions that the administration was effectively conceding the war to the communists.

A fragment in Robert Caro's *The Passage of Power* captures Johnson's determination to keep Vietnam simmering. In March, McGeorge Bundy with some exasperation, asked Johnson, "What is your own internal thinking on this, Mr. President?"

Johnson replied: "I just can't believe that we can't take 15,000 [*sic*] advisers and 200,000 people [South Vietnamese troops] and maintain the *status quo* for six months. I just believe we can do that, if we do it right."

Bundy's biographer Gordon Goldstein writes in *Lessons in Disaster* that there was a "litany of nondecisions" in 1964—"the decision *not* to withdraw, *not* to escalate, *not* to neutralize, *not* to debate the domino theory, and, fatefully, *not* to examine the military limitations and implications of a massive deployment of U.S ground combat forces to South Vietnam." In Bundy's mind, Goldstein concludes, politics became "the enemy of strategy" and the justification for official indecision and public deception.

McNamara's position was unique among the senior advisers as the Johnson administration settled in. As a recognized family intimate of the Kennedys, he had to straddle his emotions about that and Johnson's feelings about Jackie and Bobby while adapting his continuing role as secretary of defense to a vastly different person in the Oval Office.

McNamara writes in *In Retrospect:*

> Between his ascendency to the presidency and my departure from the Pentagon, President Johnson and I developed the strongest possible bonds of mutual respect and affection. However, our relationship was different from the one I had with President Kennedy, and more complicated. Johnson was a rough individual, rough on his friends as well as his enemies. He took every person's measure. He sought to find a person's weakness, and once he found it, he tried to play on it. He could be a bully, though he was never that way with me. He learned that I would deal straight with him, telling

him what I believed rather than I thought he wanted to hear, but also that once he, as the president, made a decision, I would do all in my power to carry it out.

In our transcripts, however, McNamara portrayed aspects of the relationship in another way. With the buildup in Vietnam underway in 1965, McNamara recommended a tax increase to pay the cost.
I said to Johnson, in effect, "That's going to be inflationary, we have to have a tax increase."
And Johnson said, "Where's your vote count?"
I said, ". . . get your own damn vote count."
He said, "You get your ass up there and get your vote count."
So, I make an effort and I get the vote count and I come back . . . Sure, I knew when I recommended it, [it] would be difficult. But I said I would rather try and fail than not at all. It's the right thing to do.
[LBJ then responded,] *"That's what's wrong with you, Bob, you don't know a goddamned thing about politics."*

Bullseye. McNamara's technocratic acuity and demonstrated willingness to carry out presidential edicts was not matched by political judgment and measured public style. The result was his reputation for bombastic recitation of the facts, which he privately understood was a presentation flaw but could not modify.

Nuance in managing public perception was a Kennedy skill, and political savvy was Johnson's. McNamara had neither.

Over 1964 and 1965, most of the Kennedy senior team left the administration. Bundy gradually found dealing with Johnson too hard. Ted Sorensen, the exceptional wordsmith, could not overcome his grief over Kennedy's death. Press secretary Pierre Salinger, resident historian Arthur Schlesinger Jr., the political team from Boston all moved on, to be replaced by LBJ's choices—Jack Valenti, Walter Jenkins, and Bill Moyers, among others.

There were changes as well among the Joint Chiefs, and Ambassador Lodge in Saigon was replaced by General Maxwell Taylor. However, one leading official, Dean Rusk, stayed on, serving until the end of Johnson's term in 1969—and that may have been an underestimated aspect of all that was to go wrong.

With his editors, McNamara explained his view of how government worked and how that contributed to what he considered an awkward "dynamic" in the administration:

I think the American public and cabinet officers and residents don't understand the government. They don't understand there's only one—leave out the vice president—there's only one elected official in the Executive Branch. Every other person in the Executive Branch is appointed by the president ... They have no independent power base ...

I didn't believe I had independent power. This is one of the things that affected the way I behaved as secretary, particularly during Vietnam.

McNamara's definition of his role was never under any circumstances to undermine the people's choice for the nation's highest office—yet another reason that he subsumed his views on the war into Johnson's quest for a validating election victory in 1964 and beyond. As secretary of defense and within his own limitations, McNamara carried out his role effectively.

That was clearly not the case with Secretary of State Dean Rusk. Though McNamara was adamant that he would not criticize Rusk personally in his book, nonetheless the portrayal of Rusk that emerges is negative. (Rusk died in 1994 before the book was published and while the writing was underway.) McNamara writes, "It was not a secret that President Kennedy was deeply dissatisfied with Dean Rusk's administration of the State Department" but did not make a change, nor did Johnson.

In October 1964, Undersecretary of State George Ball, who was singular in his opposition to the Johnson administration's Vietnam policy, sent a sixty-two-page memorandum which McNamara describes as remarkable for its "depth, breadth, and iconoclasm." The memo was sent to Rusk, Bundy, and McNamara but did not reach Johnson, although in 1964 it probably wouldn't have made a difference.

With his editors, and reflecting his appraisal of Rusk as ineffectual, McNamara asked rhetorically, *Where the hell was Dean? Here's this guy who's [under]secretary of state, saying we ought to get out and the goddamned memo didn't even get to the president. And the view wasn't raised. What in the hell was he doing running the State Department like that?*

McNamara said that while he disagreed with Ball's arguments, *I would have forwarded the memo to the President and said, "This is what ... my deputy and he's totally wrong and here's why. But I want you to know that view exists." And we would have debated it ...*

Now, that was Dean. And I've got to say this in a way that brings out the truth about Dean and yet doesn't shaft him ... Dean should have brought it to the president. And by God, if he didn't ... I should have.

McNamara thought the Ball memo was important enough to return to it repeatedly as work on the memoir progressed. Ball's opposition to the strategies put forward for Vietnam was the only serious high-level argument made against greater involvement. As the escalation decisions were discussed in 1965, Ball was again outspoken in opposition.

Rusk's tenure was a reflection of Washington culture in the 1960s, which was still in the early stages of the use of leaks, asides, and rumors to demean White House staff and cabinet members. Even so, Rusk considered himself vulnerable.

McNamara was so astonished by one episode in the summer of 1967 that he included it in the book despite its personal nature:

> Dean phoned me one hot afternoon to ask if he could come to my office. I told him the secretary of state does not come to the

secretary of defense's office; it is the other way around. "No, no," he said, "it's a personal matter." I said I did not care whether it was personal or official business—I would be in his office in fifteen minutes.

When I arrived, he pulled a bottle of whiskey out of his desk drawer, poured a drink for himself, and said, "I must resign."

"You're insane," I said. "What are you talking about?"

He said his daughter planned to marry a black classmate at Stanford University, and he could not impose such a political burden on the president ... He believed that because he was a southerner, working for a southern president, such a marriage—if he did not resign or stop it—would bring down immense criticism on both him and the president.

When I asked him if he had talked to the president, he said no, he did not wish to burden him.

"Burden him hell!" I said. "You'll really burden him if you resign. And I know he won't permit it. If you won't talk to the president, I will."

Johnson's reaction was to congratulate Rusk on the

marriage. The incident showed Rusk's personal awkwardness, which doubtless was one of the reasons his influence on Vietnam was so vexed.

In 1966, when George Ball left the State Department, Attorney General Nicholas Katzenbach accepted a demotion to become undersecretary of state, which was recognition that the department needed better management than Rusk could provide.

At the end of the Johnson years, McNamara told his editors, while he was at the World Bank and McGeorge Bundy was at the Ford Foundation, Rusk could not find a job. *Why did [Rusk] go to the University of Georgia? Hell ... because he couldn't get accepted anywhere else.*

For all that, McNamara considered Rusk "*a great American*," an especially vivid example of one of the men who served Kennedy and then Johnson to his maximum capacity and nonetheless ended with a reputation in tatters and a career culminating in failure.

Rusk and McNamara led the departments with the operational responsibility for Vietnam. McGeorge Bundy as national security adviser was the third top-tier official, but without the administrative burden of a cabinet member. Bundy filled his role in every respect but one, and that was defining—his failure to help LBJ avoid the Vietnam abyss. Bundy's role at Harvard, his pedigree and presence made him ideal for the Kennedy team, and his standing with LBJ as a man with the coolest of trappings who showed respect for Johnson worked well for about two years.

McNamara reveals in *In Retrospect* that after JFK's death he was told by Bobby that the president had intended to replace Rusk in a second term with him. "I would have urged him to appoint Mac Bundy, whose knowledge of history, international relations, and geopolitics was far greater than mine," he writes.

Although McNamara and Bundy's policy role in the escalation were comparable, historians and pundits have not portrayed Bundy with the degree of animus that McNamara has received. That was, in my view, because of Bundy's generally lighter touch in all dealings with others in the administration and the media. His long tenure as president of the Ford Foundation was recognized as a paragon of progressive philanthropy.

McNamara's years at the World Bank were disparaged as an effort at redemption.

Gordon Goldstein, the author of *Lessons in Disaster*, says that Bundy's never-completed memoir would have been as full of rueful explanations as *In Retrospect*. Bundy seemed to understand that he had been spared ignominy. The Bundy manuscript, such as it was, may someday be released and will make that clear.

★ ★ ★ ★ ★

The spring and summer of the election year moved on two tracks, which was to be the historical paradox of the Johnson presidency: Vietnam, where Johnson was flailing, and the Great Society, his domestic policy ambitions that were a genuine, deeply felt priority.

"Amid all this uncertainty and frustrating confusion, I made an impulsive and ill-considered public statement that has dogged me ever since," McNamara writes in a particularly revealing passage in his memoir. At a Pentagon briefing on April 24, this was the answer when a reporter said that Senator Wayne Morse of Oregon, a staunch critic of the administration's Vietnam policy, had called the conflict "McNamara's war."

"I am following the President's policy," McNamara responded. " ... I must say [in that sense] I don't object to its being called McNamara's War. I think it is a very important war and I am pleased to be identified with it and do whatever I can to win it."

Less than a week later, talking to Johnson, McNamara's tone was altogether different. LBJ asked, "Have we got anybody that's got a military mind that can give us some military plans for winning that war?" McNamara mentioned General Earle (Bus) Wheeler, who would be appointed chairman of the Joint Chiefs of Staff in July to replace Maxwell Taylor, who was being sent to Vietnam to replace Henry Cabot Lodge Jr., all meant to shore up the "mess" in Saigon, as it was being called in any number of private conversations.

McNamara recalled his conversation with the president about Wheeler's recent trip to Vietnam:

LBJ: He came back with planes, that's all he had in mind ...

McNamara: Well, uh, yes we had more than that, but he emphasized planes ...

LBJ: Let's get more of something, my friend, because I'm going to have a heart attack if you don't get me something. I'm just sitting here every day and, uh, and this war ... I'm not doing much about fightin' it and, uh, I'm not doing much about winnin' it ... Let's get somebody that wants to do something besides drop a bomb, but go in and take these damn fellas and run them back where they belong ...

But when U.S. combat options were put forward, Johnson rejected them, and his advisers couldn't suggest any coherent alternatives.

On May 22, in a commencement speech at the University of Michigan, Johnson framed his vision for the Great Society to "enrich and elevate our national life." The goal—an affirmation of the highest aspirations of the Declaration of Independence—was to eradicate poverty, inequality, and injustice.

"But most of all," Johnson said, as his rhetoric soared, "the Great Society is not a safe harbor, a resting place, a final objective, a finished work. It is a challenge constantly renewed, beckoning us toward a destiny where the meaning of our lives matches the marvelous products of our labor."

It may well have been impossible to reconcile these two tracks. Facing the reality in Vietnam, as McNamara came to believe, would mean accepting JFK's ingrained belief that unless the South Vietnamese could demonstrate their own capacity to prevail politically and militarily, the U.S. could not do it for them. Yet in 1964, stating this unequivocally was never going to happen.

The U.S. had departed, in McNamara's words, from the *"fundamental principles that Kennedy had premised our intervention on without recognizing ourselves that we departed from them."* And so the Johnson administration was inexorably overtaken by events and the continuing contention that withdrawal or neutralization—as President Charles de Gaulle of France was advocating—would be considered unacceptable defeat.

When the decision was made to replace Lodge in Saigon, McNamara volunteered for the job. Johnson did not consider this, but at one point the president asked McNamara if he would agree to serve as vice president on the 1964 ticket. "Knowing President Johnson as I did," McNamara writes, "I knew that if I answered yes, he might later reconsider and withdraw the invitation. In any event, I said no."

Over the summer, Johnson said he wanted McNamara to be his "number one executive vice president in charge of the Cabinet" in the next term.

In words private and public, LBJ and McNamara were to be inextricable going forward in how the war would be perceived.

★ ★ ★ ★ ★

In the decade of America's Vietnam war, there were pivotal events that forecast the outcome. The November

1963 coup against Diem and Nhu and the political chaos that followed was certainly one such event. The Tonkin Gulf incidents of August 1964 were another. While minimal in actual warfare they became the baseline for what would transpire thereafter.

The details of the Tonkin Gulf incidents of late July and early August 1964 are straightforward enough. A covert South Vietnamese operation codenamed Plan 34A involved the infiltration of South Vietnamese agents with radios into the north and the use of hit-and-run attacks on North Vietnamese shore and island installations—in other words, a minor but direct assault on the North. The CIA supported these operations, and the U.S. military kept track of them.

At the same time, the United States had deployed patrols in the region (known as DESOTO patrols) as part of a global reconnaissance operation using specially equipped naval vessels to collect information that might be useful in any military confrontation with adversaries. Plan 34A and DESOTO were entirely separate. McNamara writes, "Most of the South Vietnamese agents sent into North Vietnam were either captured or killed, and the seaborne attacks amounted to little more than pinpricks ... The South Vietnamese government saw them as a relatively low-cost means of harassing North Vietnam."

On August 2, the two operations intersected when the U.S. destroyer *Maddox*, on DESOTO patrol, came into contact with North Vietnamese vessels firing torpedoes and automatic weapons—Hanoi's retaliation for the Plan 34A activities a few days before. It was a summer weekend and McNamara, as he said, was in Newport visiting Jackie Kennedy. Bundy was on Martha's Vineyard doing what LBJ derisively described as "playing tennis at the *female* island."

The U.S. had sanctioned Plan 34A, so the North Vietnamese assault on the *Maddox* was not really unprovoked.

"Well," said Johnson, "it reminds me of the movies in Texas. You're sitting next to a pretty girl, and you have your hand on her ankle, and nothing happens. And you move it up to her knee and nothing happens. And you move it up further and you're thinking about moving a bit more and all of a sudden you get slapped. I think we got slapped."

With that earthy quip, Johnson concluded that the episode was not a pretext for a military response—although it was later made clear that the attack on the *Maddox* had been ordered in Hanoi. A note of protest was sent to Hanoi asserting that the incident had been "unprovoked," although Plan 34A was in fact a provocation while DESOTO was technically not one.

On August 4, the *Maddox* returned to the Gulf of Tonkin accompanied by another U.S. destroyer, the USS *Turner Joy*. The *Maddox* reported that it was preparing for an imminent attack on a cloudy night with thunderstorms. The transcripts of radio traffic that night reveal (and what history has concluded) is that no actual attack on the U.S.

ships ever took place, although something might have happened. Being unresolved, the consensus has become that the episode was a misrepresentation of the facts, which in the overall saga was considered deliberate deception rather than confusion.

What makes that judgment significant is that the Tonkin Gulf Resolution the administration put forward and passed unanimously by the House and 88-2 by the Senate on August 7, gave LBJ enormous power to pursue his objectives in Vietnam. It is also clear that no one anticipated that the authority approved after a minor incident in offshore waters would morph into a half million American combat troops and a sustained bombing campaign that would go on for years.

Johnson's political strategy for 1964 was vindicated by his sweeping victory over Goldwater in the general election. He continued to stress moderation in his public statements and American "moral" purpose in helping the "weak defend their freedom."

Yet whenever he gathered his military and political advisers, proposals went round and round without reaching tactical outcomes that could be implemented.

McNamara told his editors assessing what he wanted to say about that period:

The Chiefs were much more divided than anybody understood and ... there was a distinct failure—I don't want to put it quite that bluntly, but there was a distinct failure of military leadership....

There's one place in here where I say, I failed ... For fifty years, I've been a manager. For fifty years I dealt with organization. I know how to probe and penetrate and not accept things that are presented to me. I didn't do it here. It's my failure.

So, at the end of Lyndon Johnson's first year as president, with the mandate of leadership that he wanted so badly, the men who surrounded him were divided among themselves, whether always deliberately or not, misleading the public, exaggerating the prospect of Soviet or Chinese direct intervention in the war and about to launch the escalation that—as they understood—was almost certainly hopeless.

Chapter Three
Escalation 1965
★ ★ ★

PRESIDENT JOHNSON'S INAUGURAL on a cold January 20, 1965, in Washington should have been the pinnacle of his ascendance to power and glory, his life objectives. But his demeanor was solemn.

After a year of sustained and inconclusive deliberations, the options for delay in Vietnam had run out. The issue was being framed in two ways.

On one side was this perspective: The South Vietnamese would have to show a capacity to wage a successful war against North Vietnam and the Vietcong, as President Kennedy believed. Absent that, the United States should proceed with a gradual withdrawal of advisers and absorb the political consequences, even if that meant that the dreaded "dominos" would fall.

The earlier deliberations over neutrality for Laos and the decision to use diplomacy over force in the Cuban missile crisis had persuaded JFK, from the evidence in Robert McNamara's reflections, that there were alternatives to using air power or combat troops to forestall what would still eventually be a defeat.

As McNamara told his editors:

You can't create a nation by military means. ... Kennedy believed two things that I don't think others may have accepted when he said them—and he didn't put it quite as forcefully as I'm going to ... There are two absolute fundamental requirements to save Vietnam. One is political stability, and the other is a South Vietnamese capacity to defend themselves.

The opposing view, expressed by, among others, former President Eisenhower, was that the United States could not allow a communist takeover in another Asian country. They rejected the analogy of Vietnam to a neutralized Laos or to the stable if uneasy ceasefire on the Korean peninsula. Instead, they were convinced that Chinese and Soviet support for the North Vietnamese was a significant threat to America's role in the world.

Ultimately Johnson came to reluctantly accept that American "boys" would have to be deployed to defeat the enemy. And in the first six months of 1965, McNamara and Bundy joined Rusk in reaching the same conclusion, and the Joint Chiefs began to implement the ground and air strategy.

Moreover, Johnson may well have also felt that his landslide victory over Barry Goldwater in the 1964 presidential election had given him the leeway to use force that he expected—and was told—would turn around the situation.

On January 27, 1965, just days after the inauguration, McNamara and Bundy delivered a memorandum to the president that portrayed the situation in Vietnam in stark terms: a moment of choosing had come, and Johnson had to decide whether to proceed with a direct U.S. military intervention or a withdrawal of American advisers, leading to a negotiated resolution to the conflict. It became known as the "Fork in the Road" memo.

As McNamara later told his editors:

In early January, the Vietcong mauled two elite South Vietnamese units in major battles. Combined with intelligence reports the North Vietnamese army regulars had begun entering the South ... South Vietnam seemed on the brink of total collapse. These events made me conclude, painfully and reluctantly, that the time had come to change course.

Still, while the memo presented withdrawal and negotiations as an option, McNamara and Bundy told the president that they favored increasing military engagement.

McNamara and Bundy might still have moved toward the Kennedy approach if Johnson had made that choice. He was the president and they were advisers, as both would later insist in explanation.

One of the most striking discoveries in accounts of the period comes in Lady Bird's diaries, her regular and very private description of what went on day to day.

On February 11, in the midst of a chatty report on her activities, she wrote:

While Lyndon and [Vice President] Hubert [Humphrey] were talking I was startled to hear him say something I had heard so often but did not really expect to come out of his mouth in front of anyone else. "I'm not temperamentally equipped to be Commander-in-Chief," he said. They were talking about the crisis in Vietnam and the long nights with phone calls about planes going out and casualties, the necessity of giving orders, that would produce, God knows what cataclysmic results.

He said, "I'm too sentimental to give the orders!" Somehow I could not wish him not to hurt when he gives the orders.

When Humphrey turned out (in the parlance of the time) to be a "dove" on the war, LBJ excluded him from the deliberations, perhaps recognizing that his vice president knew more about the president's distress than he wanted to share with others. Humphrey had endorsed a memo written with Thomas Hughes, a former aide who was at the State Department, calling for withdrawal, which landed without impact.

As a former vice president himself, LBJ knew what it meant to be frozen out of presidential decision making. Still, he never gave Humphrey the influence he craved.

Between the "Fork in the Road" memo and July 1965, the United States launched the "Rolling Thunder" air campaign, which over the ensuing years dropped the largest amount of bombs in history on the enemy. The Johnson administration also authorized the deployment of 175,000 combat troops to South Vietnam.

As momentum for escalation increased the main proponent of restraint was George Ball, who was Rusk's deputy at the State Department. In memos and meetings, he argued that bombs and combat presence would not work, given the factors on the battlefield and in North Vietnam. Supporting Ball was Clark Clifford, who had no official position in the administration but was an adviser to LBJ, using his reputation and experience to make a case whenever he had the opportunity.

In *Counsel to the President*, Clifford includes a letter he wrote to Johnson on May 17, 1965:

> I wish to make one major point.
>
> I believe our ground forces in South Vietnam should be kept to a minimum consistent with the protection of our installations and property in that country. My concern is that a substantial buildup of U.S. ground troops would be construed by the Communists, and by the world, as a determination on our part to win the war on the ground.

> This could be a quagmire. It could turn into an open ended commitment on our part that would take more and more ground troops, without a realistic hope of ultimate victory.

Clifford says he did not get a reply.

As their editor, I never tried to have McNamara and Clifford reconcile their positions, which not surprisingly differed in their sense of impact. McNamara carried the responsibility of overseeing the Pentagon, whereas Clifford's role as an adviser would have no direct consequences, even if he wanted to think that it did.

On June 21, there was a meeting in the Cabinet Room that included all the official advisers and, in the afternoon, Clifford. (Historians say that Clifford's account of the session elevates his presence beyond what the transcript of the session shows it to be. The gist, however, is correct.)

"Everyone in the room seemed deeply aware," Clifford recounts, "that we were facing—belatedly in my opinion—a momentous decision. Westmoreland had requested thirty-two additional American combat battalions—100,000 more men by the end of the year, *more* in 1966, plus an intensification of the bombing of the North and a partial mobilization of the National Guard and the Reserves ...

When I entered, George Ball was speaking. 'We can't win,' he said ... 'The war will be long and protracted, with heavy casualties. The most we can hope for is a messy conclusion ... '

"One by one, the other senior members of the Administration lined up against Ball."

Ball had submitted a lengthy memo (the one that never reached Johnson) arguing against American intervention. In McNamara's view, one factor that contributed to the memo's weakness was that it stopped short of saying that withdrawal with all of its fallout was better than staying:

[Ball] couldn't bring himself to say in that sixty-two-page memo, "I accept that getting out will lead to all these [global political] problems, but that's better than the problems we'll face staying in." That memo doesn't say that.

On July 25 at Camp David, LBJ convened McNamara, Clifford, and several of his closest personal advisers like Jack Valenti and Bill Moyers for the weekend. There was a meeting of principals portrayed as a final argument for and against the full mandate for escalation. McNamara was to argue for and Clifford against the expansion.

Valenti took notes. Moyers's view was that as press secretary, it was not his role to promote one policy or another. (To this day, Moyers has never shared his views on the war.)

When it was over, LBJ went off by himself. Clifford believed that this was when the president finally and conclusively decided to go all in, whatever it would take. I asked Clifford in an editorial session how it felt to be on the losing side of so consequential a debate. As a litigator, he said, it was his role to make his argument, accept the outcome and move on.

(Clifford's book *Counsel to the President* was published in 1991, before he was indicted in a banking scandal—though he was never tried. By the mid-1990s, McNamara's description of Clifford's role in the Vietnam deliberations had a tone of condescension, in contrast to Clifford's own depiction, which had emphasized his gravitas.)

As the war progressed, Clifford became an advocate of more military pressure to prevail. By the fall of 1967, Clifford had concluded that that the United States should find a way to disengage. Once he became secretary of defense he began to press for negotiated withdrawal and peace talks.

McGeorge Bundy, working with Gordon Goldstein, describes that period and those deliberations with a somewhat different emphasis. In *Lessons in Disaster,* Bundy recounts his relative "passivity" as the argument progressed as his "worst failure." Quoting from a draft fragment written by Bundy, Goldstein conveys that the former national security adviser felt that he was wrong "not to press the study of the prospects of success, of one side's strength and one side's weakness, especially in 1965. Not to examine what could be done to make the best of a bad business while not escalating."

Goldstein adds that this was the essential irony of Bundy's role in the Johnson White House: "In response to the crisis in Vietnam, the administration's preeminent intellectual demonstrated a fundamental lack of rigor in his analysis of the ends and means of American strategy."

Bundy had, if anything, a more limited view of his role in the process. By the spring of 1965, he said, he considered himself a "staff officer who knows the big decision is made and is working to help in its execution."

That view encompasses another aspect of the 1965 deliberations: Johnson's use of his consultations with his advisers as a means of showing that he was considering all sides of the case, while actually and privately coming to accept Westmoreland's—and by now, McNamara's—plan for expanding troop strength.

While Clifford's account presents the Camp David session as climactic, it was in fact only the last piece of LBJ's balancing of something he had already concluded he had to do in way that would in his own mind justify reversing his stance from 1964, as a candidate, with the decisions he was making in 1965. Of that period, McNamara writes in a closing sentence of his chapter on escalation decisions, "We were sinking into quicksand."

Those decisions and the way they were presented to the American public shaped the rest of the Vietnam war, and in its way, as important, they created a lasting breach with the American people over trust in government. Inherent suspicion of the messages and motives that have come from succeeding administrations are a corrosive factor in political debates and democratic principles.

Beginning with the initial decisions on a bombing strategy and deployment in February 1965, Johnson chose not to tell the American people what he knew to be the case: that the war was entering a very different stage. That month Bundy had delivered a memo to the president following his first trip to Vietnam, where he was shocked by an attack in the Highlands in which some American advisers were killed. In Bundy's memo, as McNamara recalled, the message was this:

"At its very best the struggle in Vietnam will be long. It seems to us important that this fundamental fact be made clear and our understanding of it be made clear to our own people."

In his book, McNamara adds: "As I will relate, it was not."

He went on to recount that "President Johnson finally decided on February 19 that regular strikes against the North would begin, but he again refused Mac's advice to announce the decision publicly." At the time polls showed that a significant majority of Americans supported the war policies, without knowing they were being changed. "These numbers, McNamara writes, "changed dramatically over the next three years, as Johnson's continued lack of candor steadily diminished popular faith in his credibility and leadership."

McNamara recalls that with majority support in the country for escalation, LBJ had the opportunity to be forthcoming with the public, as he was urged to do by liberals among his advisers, including Douglas Cater, formerly an editor at *The Reporter* magazine, and John Gardner, his secretary of health, education and welfare.

Those two guys are liberals, and they said to Johnson, ... "Mr. President, you've got to expose more ... the people are with you. Take them into your confidence. They want you to do what you want to do."

Johnson's successes in closing deals on Capitol Hill tended toward backroom bargaining and tradeoffs, which was different from publicly explaining the decision to fight a losing war. McNamara told his editors that the reason for his own contributions to misleading the public was:

For me to go public and say we weren't winning ... for anybody—if the president went public and said, "We're not winning," because it was a fact in the midst of a war, that is a hell of a thing to say.

He added that when the escalation began, the military in particular were predicating its recommendations on the assumption that with enough force victory would be possible, if not certain. McNamara may well have thought the generals could be right, even though he clearly doubted they were.

In a speech at Johns Hopkins University on April 7, 1965, answering his own rhetorical question, "Why are we in South Vietnam?" Johnson reiterated American promises to support the Saigon government, a pledge made by Presidents Eisenhower and Kennedy and the commitment to "strengthen world order" against Communist incursions.

He said that in response to stepped-up attacks in South Vietnam, air strikes were underway—but he did not mention ground deployments. "This is not a change of purpose. It is a change in what we believe that purpose requires."

And LBJ quoted scripture: "We must say in Southeast Asia as we did in Europe in the words of the Bible: 'Hitherto shalt thou come but no further.'"

McNamara, Bundy, and Clifford, each in his way, attribute Johnson's vagueness and prevarications to aspects of his character. For as long as possible, he did not want Vietnam to undermine his Great Society agenda, either by warning the public about trouble ahead or by going to Congress with requests for the real costs that the war would entail.

When McNamara urged LBJ to raise taxes to meet the additional costs of war, that was when the president had told his defense secretary that he just didn't understand politics. Which was, of course, the case.

McNamara also concluded, as he told his editors, that Johnson believed that *"the end justifies the means"* and if he was able to succeed in his domestic reforms and reverse the slide in Vietnam, his lack of candor about the war would be overlooked or forgotten.

Johnson also believed that if he were to announce incremental, if open ended, moves in the war, he would come under pressure from conservatives—the "hawks"— to go further and faster. Ironically, Johnson's politically motivated effort to order not too much escalation—or to do so too publicly—would lead to battlefield frustration and his political demise.

While there were minor feints aimed at a diplomatic approach with North Vietnam, none of which came to anything, Johnson was also stymied, he said, by the absence of any plan to end the war by negotiations, without victory or defeat. At one meeting in July, he said, as quoted by Clifford, "This war is like a prizefight. Our right hand is our military power, but our left hand must be peace proposals. Every time you move troops forward, you should move diplomats forward, too. I want this done. The Generals want more and more from me. They want to go farther and farther. But State has to supply me with something, too."

Rusk, who heard the complaint, did not reply. George Ball's counsel, with Clifford's support, had been rejected.

In *Lessons in Disaster*, Gordon Goldstein writes of McGeorge Bundy, "Frustrated by a deteriorating relationship with President Johnson"—in ways other than the Vietnam issues—"he was on the precipice of resigning as national security adviser." Bundy then agreed to appear on a prime-time television debate on CBS on the evening of June 21, without telling Johnson.

On the program, Bundy fared poorly in defending the administration's Vietnam policy before a panel of five respected scholars. As a consequence, he found himself in the untenable and ultimately unsustainable position of falling out with his peers and then with Johnson. After that—as Vietnam controversies in the administration, teach-ins on campuses and a distraction of political upheaval in the Dominican Republic went on—Bundy became essentially irrelevant in real decision making.

When he finally left to join the Ford Foundation in 1966, he was replaced by Walt Rostow, his deputy, an unequivocal hawk, who was to stay until the end of LBJ's term.

The top echelons of the military, from all historical accounts, continued to be divided over strategy and was never really able, then or later, to reach conclusions that were as clear as they should have been.

H. R. McMaster's book *Dereliction of Duty: Johnson, McNamara, the Joint Chiefs of Staff, and the Lies that Led to Vietnam*, published in 1997, is devastating in its criticism: "The failing were many and reinforcing arrogance, weakness, lying in pursuit of self-interest and above all, the abdication of responsibility to the American people." A career army officer who later rose to the rank of lieutenant general (and briefly served as Donald Trump's national security adviser), he calls his chapter about the Joint Chiefs in July 1965 "Five Silent Men."

LBJ's emotional trajectory comes through his own copious transcribed record, but Lady Bird's diaries, as described in more than one hundred hours of her tapes and Julia Sweig's book *Lady Bird Johnson: Hiding in Plain Sight*, comes as close as possible to portraying her husband's downward spin as the war progressed.

Before the Camp David weekend in July, she wrote about her sleep problems as Lyndon faced the decisions that he would have to make on Vietnam: "For an extraordinarily healthy, tough, reasonably happy person, sleeping is becoming the hardest thing for me to do, particularly when I feel that I have not played my role well, that I have been a hindrance."

Sweig writes that Lady Bird could not console her husband, hoping that a Camp David weekend with some relaxation along with the policy discussion might help. "She'd seen time and again," Sweig writes, "how the release of tension that comes with a difficult decision could ease Lyndon's torment, self-doubt and depression."

It is of course unknowable whether in those months of 1965, as Johnson was coming to his fateful decision to send in troops and bombers, he might have made a different choice. He was being pressured to do so by all and sundry—often with conflicting and confusing advice—and even though his telephone tapes often expressed frustration and doubts that escalation could ultimately succeed, he went ahead.

As McNamara underscored to his editors:

The divisions among us and the unresolvable nature of our objectives continued though and beyond my departure from the Pentagon.

An exaggerated belief in the Soviet and Chinese threat to American power, ignorance about the true nature of the conflict and competing egos and strategies of military, civilian and political advisers, combined with LBJ's own deeply embedded ambitions for domestic change and his insecurities about appearing weak in a foreign conflict, were the toxic brew that produced the Vietnam debacle, which now everywhere is deemed a tragedy.

★ ★ ★ ★ ★

On the battlefield, the impact of American forces was being felt in direct conflict with the Vietcong. Even Bernard Fall, an eminent French expert on Vietnam (considered a particular sage by many press pundits, including I. F. Stone, whose weekly newsletter was a leader in challenging American forecasts of the war), wrote in *Newsweek* that U.S. power might make a decisive difference—an opinion he would later abandon, shortly before his death two years later, when he was killed by a roadside bomb in Vietnam.

And the effect of the escalation on the ground turned out to be short-lived. In the summer and fall of 1965, McNamara writes in *In Retrospect*, "reality collided with expectations. We no sooner had begun to carry out the plan to increase dramatically U.S. forces in Vietnam than it became clear there was reason to question the strategy on which the plan was based. Slowly, the sobering, frustrating limitations of military operations became painfully apparent. I had always been confident that every problem could be solved, but now I found myself confronting one—involving national pride and human life—that could not.

"My sense of the war gradually shifted from concern to skepticism to frustration to anguish. It shifted not because of growing fatigue, as was sometimes alleged, but because of my increasing anxiety that more and more people were being killed and we simply were not accomplishing our goals."

Strikingly in all the documentation of this period, the issue of the war's morality—the deaths of so many South Vietnamese civilians—was never the overriding concern. Criticism of the war inside the administration was about tactics and strategy—and the political costs of giving up—not about how to justify so much violence for a worst-case projection of the risks of communism across Asia.

On November 2 came another pivotal event in the wartime narrative, the self-immolation of Norman Morrison, a young Quaker, father of three, in front of the Pentagon and just yards from McNamara's office window. Campus teach-ins and commentary in the press opposing escalation had little of the emotional impact of Morrison's death—an echo of the Buddhist monks' immolations that preceded the ouster of Diem in November 1963. Morrison's family released a statement that he had given his life "over the great loss of life and human suffering caused by the war in Vietnam."

McNamara writes: "I reacted to the horror of his action by bottling up my emotions and avoided talking them with anyone—even my family. I knew Marg and our three children shared many of Morrison's feelings about the war ... And I believed I understood and shared some of his thoughts. There was much Marg and I and the children should have talked about, yet at moments like this I often turn inward instead—it is a grave weakness. The episode created tension at home that only deepened as dissent and criticism of the war continued to grow."

In May 2022, McNamara's son, Craig, published a book called *Because Our Fathers Lied: A Memoir of Truth and Family, from Vietnam to Today*. The title implies more malice than Robert McNamara, by his own account, intended. His personality and his official role led him and others around LBJ—including the president himself—repeatedly to sublimate moral judgment to strategy.

There were other ironies that autumn. Clashes in Kashmir, in which the Chinese-backed Pakistanis took up arms against Soviet-aligned India highlighted the split between the two major communist powers. And in Indonesia, the Communist Party (supported by China) launched an unsuccessful coup; as many as a half million party members were massacred. Suharto, an independent nationalist, came to power.

After the failed coup, McNamara recalled, a "bellicose and aggressive" speech by the Chinese defense minister, Lin Biao, "seemed to us a clear expression of the basis for the domino theory," even though the foreign policy expert George F. Kennan argued that China had "suffered an enormous reverse in Indonesia ... one of great significance and one that rather confines any realistic hopes they may have for expansion of their authority." Kennan's misunderstood Cold War advocacy of "containment" of Soviet power (he felt that the USSR could be contained because of its post-World War II weaknesses, not because of its strengths) had become the justification for the anti-communist crusades around the world. At a Senate hearing in February 1966, Kennan testified that there were now fewer dominoes in Asia to fall. "Kennan's point failed to catch our attention and thus influence our actions," McNamara writes.

McNamara's next major initiative in policy came in an options memo he sent the president in November, after another trip to Vietnam. On leaving Saigon, he remarked to reporters: "We have stopped losing the war ... But despite the fact that we've had that success, ... [the Vietcong and North Vietnamese] have more than offset the very heavy losses which they have suffered. The level of infiltration has increased, and I think this represents a clear decision on the part of Hanoi to ... raise the level of conflict."

In his memo, McNamara offered LBJ two options— essentially the same choices that he and Bundy had been putting forward all year: more escalation, fulfilling General Westmoreland's request for a sharp increase in force power, or a renewed effort at finding a path to negotiation. Back in the spring, Dean Rusk had surprised the Soviet ambassador to the United States, Anatoly Dobrynin, with what Dobrynin in his memoir *In Confidence* called a "peace feeler ... in the most tentative, unofficial, and personal manner."

As a diplomat, Dobrynin, whose time in Washington encompassed six presidential administrations, dealt primarily with Rusk, and he characterized those exchanges as serious but civil disagreement. At a State Department reception in May, Rusk, "emphasizing that neither the United States nor the Soviet Union should be enslaved by its own partners" in Vietnam, "gave me to understand that our countries might join forces (without publicizing it) to reach a stage-by-stage settlement."

Dobrynin elaborated: "Suppose, he said, a confidential agreement on Vietnam could be reached privately between Washington and Moscow. The United States would not regard it as a challenge if the Soviet Union simultaneously gave North Vietnam a solemn military guarantee against American bombardment. On the whole, the developments might look like a compromise reached in the face of imminent confrontation between the two superpowers. This, among other things, would be a major setback for China."

Rusk even suggested, according to Dobrynin, that "air raids against North Vietnam" could be halted for "a limited probation period."

In Moscow, the Soviet foreign minister, Andrei Gromyko, after a short period of consideration made it clear that there would be no negotiation.

That also was to be the view in Washington when McNamara again put forward a negotiation notion in November. But the idea of a bombing halt, which was called a "pause," did gain support. Rusk, one of the administration's hawks, said he was behind it, perhaps because of his interactions with Dobrynin.

In December, while LBJ was at his Texas ranch recovering from gall bladder surgery, McNamara directly pressed the concept of a Christmas pause. McNamara reports in *In Retrospect* that he had grown "more and more convinced that we ought definitely to think of some action other than military action as the only program.... I personally believe we should go ahead and raise our budgets, raise our strengths [and] increase our deployments out there to gradually meet Westmoreland's requirements. But I think if we do that by itself, it's suicide and we ought definitely to accompany it—or even, perhaps, precede it—by some other action."

In an exchange in the Cabinet Room on December 17, McNamara said, "A military solution to the problem is not certain—one out of three or one in two. Ultimately we must find ... a diplomatic solution.

Johnson responded, "Then no matter what we do in the military field, there is no sure victory?"

"That's right," McNamara answered. "We have been too optimistic ... "

To which Rusk said, "I'm more optimistic, but I can't prove it."

A month earlier, Dobrynin had told Bundy at a lunch "that if the United States stopped bombing for two to three weeks, Moscow "would use its influence to get Hanoi to negotiate."

CHAPTER THREE

The bombing pause began on December 22 and was extended on a day-to-day basis. Rusk put forward a fourteen-point program soliciting North Vietnam to begin negotiations without preconditions.

Almost as soon as the bombing was stopped, the Joint Chiefs urged a resumption. And when no sign emerged of a change in Hanoi's refusal to negotiate, Johnson ordered the resumption of air attacks at the end of January 1966. McNamara quotes a Harris poll at the time that said that "the vast majority of Americans would support an immediate escalation of the war—including all-out bombings of North Vietnam and increasing U.S. troop commitments to 500,000 men."

Could the outcome of the pause have been any different? The North Vietnamese had refused to engage in negotiations. The Johnson administration was, as always, divided and therefore confused. With the Harris poll in mind, the United States went ahead and met the further demands for escalation.

So 1966 would be the year of an all-out U.S. war effort, once again in pursuit of military objectives that Johnson and McNamara understood were unlikely to meet the requirements of success.

Chapter Four
Disillusion and Delusion
★ ★ ★

BY JANUARY 1966, the United States was all-in on the war, by land, air, and sea. The Kennedy-era belief that South Vietnam could and would win its own battle had been replaced, decisively, with a strategy of American war power that in time would overwhelm the communist forces and somehow enable South Vietnam to become a bastion of democratic freedom in Asia.

Over the course of the next year, the military effort would be disappointing, at least to those who recognized that the data being compiled missed the essential point: that the North Vietnamese and the Vietcong were not yet losing the war and the South Vietnamese–U.S. alliance was not making the necessary gains.

The North Vietnamese communist leader, Ho Chi Minh, who had once identified himself with principles of the American revolution, had now become a party figurehead, and Hanoi's strategic and political strategy was now set by another communist official, Le Duan, whose name was so unfamiliar that McNamara had to spell it out for Johnson over the phone. At the same time, General Vo Nguyen Giap, the military mastermind, had lost influence to two other generals, Van Tien Dung and Hoang Van Thai, neither of whom were disposed to compromise.

In the ensuing months, there were hints of possible negotiations, approaches to which McNamara always wanted to give some credence. Still, these initiatives went nowhere. The bombing pause over the 1965 Christmas holidays ended without effect. The historian George Herring wrote years later, in his book *LBJ and Vietnam: A Different Kind of War*, that "McNamara's influence began to wane" after the bombing halt ended:

> The secretary of defense had pushed the pause and accompanying peace initiative and LBJ, grudgingly and against his better judgment, had endorsed it ... Moreover, the once indomitable secretary of defense was increasingly skeptical that the war could be won militarily ... At some point late in his tenure, he was cut off from some information because of his growing opposition to the war and his suspected ties to dovish Senator Robert Kennedy.

In *In Retrospect,* McNamara writes, "I wish Herring were right" and then asserts that while he "grew increasingly skeptical ... of our ability to achieve our political objectives in Vietnam through military means, ... this did not diminish my involvement in the shaping of Vietnam policy."

In reality, Herring's appraisal was correct in describing the trajectory of McNamara's thinking and his stature with Johnson in 1966 and into 1967.

Having launched his Great Society programs and achieved historic civil rights triumphs in Congress, LBJ wanted to link these domestic political successes with military achievements in Vietnam. In a speech at Freedom House in New York on February 23, 1966, Johnson said:

> Men who believe they can change their destinies will change their destinies. Armed with that belief they will be willing—yes, they will be eager—to make the sacrifices that freedom demands ... to become that is within them to become, to cast off the yoke of discrimination and disease; to the freedom to hope and to build on that hope, lives of integrity and well-being.
>
> That is what our struggle in Vietnam is about tonight. This is what our struggle for equal rights in this country is all about. We seek to create that climate, at home and abroad, where unlettered men can learn, where deprived children can grow, where

hopeless millions can be inspired to change the terms of their existence for the better ...

Whether in the cities and hamlets of Vietnam, or in the ghettoes of our own cities, the struggle is the same. That struggle is to end the violence against the human mind and body, so that the work of peace may be done, and the fruits of freedom may be won.

In her diaries, Lady Bird Johnson expressed a different message, as Julia Sweig points out. "She also worried about the emotional toll on Lyndon," Sweig observes, "for whom the responsibility of returning two hundred thousand American boys to safety made him feel, she thought, their collective loss even more strongly than the boys' own mothers."

Barely more than a year after the inauguration, Lady Bird recorded the following: "I count the months and the weeks until the time I have set [to exit the presidency], but I have not the force of character, and not even really the desire, to try to make Lyndon work less hard."

Another factor of consequence in 1966 was the departure of McGeorge Bundy. He and McNamara, each in his own way, had brought intellectual luster to the White House, along with their connections to the country's elites, which offset the intense rough-and-tumble of Johnson's political instincts. Although they were instrumental in devising the administration's policies in Vietnam, they could nominally identify themselves as simply developing strategy plans rather than manipulating Congress and public opinion. Those were the tactics that fostered the cynicism necessary for advisers who knew that shaping perceptions of progress was their main mission.

Bundy's departure to the Ford Foundation for the most part ended his Vietnam-related reputation—although conspiracies emerged about the foundation's connections with the CIA, never proven. Only in his never-finished memoir did Bundy's regrets surface. He described his departure to his coauthor, Gordon Goldstein, not as a break with Johnson on policy, but as differences over how that policy was presented to the public. "Once the choice of 1965 was made," Bundy recalled, "I supported it, in and out of office." Instead, he said, he was opposed "to the way the Administration, and in particular the President himself, did and did not explain" the escalation in the war.

"It was the president's lack of transparency," Goldstein writes, "that angered Bundy rather than the strategy to Americanize the war—a strategy he privately questioned with McNamara but otherwise publicly endorsed. As Bundy struggled to explain in one of his fragments, 'You must make it plain that while you wanted choices spelled out to the public, you yourself were in favor of ground combat reinforcement in 1965. You did also favor a real examination of alternatives, which did not happen.'"

McNamara, for his part, became fixated on data, a consequence of his personality and his experience and training in graduate school at Harvard and in the business world. Regarding the war in Vietnam, this meant a focus on the numbers of enemy dead and the pace of airstrikes, among other indices increasingly seen as coldly technocratic—and therefore inhumane. This stain proved to be indelible for the rest of McNamara's life.

Even McNamara's public displays of remorse, his tears when his memoir was published, were dismissed as insincere or mocked in editorial cartoons that turned what was coming from his eyes into missiles.

Errol Morris's presentation of McNamara in his Oscar-winning documentary *The Fog of War* was criticized in early reviews for letting the former secretary of defense off too easily. The closing scene of the film is an epilogue in which Morris asks McNamara whether he would specifically apologize for the war. Set off from the rest of the film (I always wondered, privately, whether it had been added after those initial reviews, which I could not confirm), the setting shows McNamara talking to Morris in a car rather than a studio.

> Morris: After you left the Johnson administration, why didn't you speak out against the Vietnam war?
>
> McNamara: I'm not going to say any more than I have. These are the kind of questions that get me in trouble. You don't

know what I know about how inflammatory my words can appear. A lot of people misunderstand the war, misunderstand me. A lot of people think I'm a son of a bitch.

Morris: Do you feel in any way responsible? Do you feel guilty?

McNamara: I don't want to go further with this discussion. It just opens up more controversy. I don't want to add anything to Vietnam. It is so complex that anything I say will require additions and qualifications.

Morris: Is it the feeling that you're damned if you do, and if you don't, no matter what?

McNamara: Yeah, that's right. And I'd rather be damned if I don't.

The data McNamara was using in his public presentations in 1966 and 1967 were diagrammed in an attrition calculation he devised and repeated, the belief that you could inflict so many casualties on the enemy that its strength would deteriorate. Westmoreland and his officers in Vietnam also adopted this rhetoric, measuring progress in the number of targets destroyed, the body counts, the traffic down the Ho Chi Minh Trail, the POWs captured, the weapons seized, and something called the Hamlet Evaluation Survey—all to make a case of progress with numbers that McNamara eventually came to understand were misleading.

Years later, in the 1980s, CBS News produced a documentary that accused Westmoreland of having systematically lied in his data. He sued the network. McNamara became entangled in explanations about how numbers gathered by the CIA could differ from those compiled by the U.S. military in Vietnam, based on who were considered combatants as distinct from village militias.

Part of the problem for McNamara was that the CBS producer of the documentary was the journalist George Crile, who, by his marriage to the daughter of the columnist Joe Alsop's wife, had been accepted in Washington social circles that were McNamara's friends even after the war, along with the Kennedys, a group known collectively as "the Georgetown set." The tag team of Crile and the CBS correspondent Mike Wallace brought celebrity panache to a case that viewers found persuasive.

McNamara told his editors that he would say, if challenged in court testimony and under oath, "*categorically ... that I do not believe it was Westmoreland's intention to deceive.*"

This cultural confusion and obfuscation resulting from LBJ's hard-edge politics, combined with the determination of Westmoreland and the Joint Chiefs to show battlefield progress, came into conflict with the emerging sense among elites in the Cambridge-Washington corridor that the war would not be won. The result was that McNamara found himself in an awkward straddle because of his association with both groups.

The Westmoreland case was eventually settled without

resolution, but the belief that McNamara was complicit if not responsible for offering up incorrect numbers never disappeared. Wallace was so upset by the trial that he had himself hospitalized for depression.

McNamara's certainty of presentation whenever he was asked to speak was a cover for his recognition that public opposition to the war was increasing—and in his own family, Marg and their offspring found it harder to balance their feelings about the war with McNamara's perceived role in it. In Craig McNamara's memoir, he recounts this dynamic that McNamara in his years of postwar reflection always wanted to deflect.

The index of *In Retrospect* shows very few references to Craig and his sisters Margy and Kathy, though the book does mention that Marg McNamara, his wife, and Craig developed severe ulcers. And when the subject of family came up in his extensive discussions with his editors, McNamara always said that he did not want to explore the topic. Craig's book made the reason as clear as it could be. The dynamic was extremely complicated.

But father and son seemed to be close. When, many years after the war, Craig and his wife embarked on becoming walnut famers in California, McNamara provided the essential funding.

As 1966 progressed, LBJ's declarations of righteous goals in Vietnam and the scale of the violence being used to support those goals were becoming irreconcilable. For his defense secretary to make the case that progress was being made and privately to recognize its weaknesses was a corrosive paradox—and enhanced what was Vietnam's legacy of mistrust and repudiation of the country's leadership.

In the spring a new round of Buddhist uprisings in the South, as McNamara writes, "underscored the Saigon government's fragility and lack of popular appeal." McNamara and John McNaughton, the Pentagon official the secretary most admired (he would have been McNamara's chosen successor had he not been killed in a plane crash in 1967) drafted a "Possible 'Fall-back' Plan" based on the belief that "while the military situation is not going badly, the political situation is in 'terminal sickness' and even the military prognosis is of an escalating stalemate."

At a White House meeting, McNamara recounts LBJ making an "elliptical remark about 'being ready to make a terrible choice—perhaps take a stand in Thailand,'" which indicated that Johnson was aware of the seriousness of the problem. "Looking back," McNamara continues, "I deeply regret that I did not force a probing debate about whether it would ever be possible to forge a winning military effort on a foundation of political quicksand."

Dean Rusk, on the other hand, was arguing that "the situation has reached the point where North Vietnam cannot succeed." Walt Rostow added, "Mr. President, you can smell it all over: Hanoi's operation backed by the Chicoms [Chinese communists] is no longer being regarded as the wave of the future ... We're not in, but we're moving."

As McNamara met with his editors and drafted chapters about the events in 1965, 1966, and 1967, he would return again and again to the factor that he came to understand underlay American determination to beat back communism—the Cold War itself:

The major lesson of the whole damn thing is we misjudged the magnitude of the communist threat, both the Soviet and Chinese threat. We misjudged them ... we overstated it ... it welded the West together, it brought unity that we wouldn't have had ... And we didn't search out contrary views.

Another irony of the period, as described by Soviet Ambassador Anatoly Dobrynin in *In Confidence*, was that his interactions with Rusk and consultations with top officials in the Kremlin always reiterated the point that the conflict in Vietnam should not mean that the United States and Soviet Union were in direct confrontation or conflict themselves or that they would be. Even though it was at war with what it contended were proxies for Moscow and Beijing, the United States also wanted to maintain outreach to the Soviets and later to Beijing (as when Nixon in 1972 traveled to China in February and then to the USSR the following June).

"Some specific questions in Soviet-American relations were solved or at least explored," Dobrynin writes. "Both governments resumed their confidential exchanges of messages and examined such ideas as the use of nuclear energy for mining and earth-moving projects, and the peaceful exploration of the moon and outer space. After a long delay we signed an agreement at the end of 1966 opening direct air traffic between the two countries."

Dobrynin also writes that the replacement of McGeorge Bundy with his deputy Walt Rostow had put an unequivocal advocate of escalation into the inner circle supporting the Joint Chiefs, who while divided among themselves on what should be done kept pressing for more commitment from their respective services.

"Johnson in fact was beginning to realize that unless the war ended in 1967," Dobrynin asserts, "he could hardly count on being reelected for another term; as the war widened, so did opposition to it across the country."

The nationally televised Senate hearings chaired by Senator William Fulbright in 1966 had an enormous impact on public opinion. "Fulbright explained to me," Dobrynin writes, "that was why the president felt that greater military pressure had to be applied to North Vietnam to force it to settle. The columnist Walter Lippmann, who increasingly and bitterly challenged the president's war policies, told me at lunch in his home early in June that Johnson and Rusk were no longer interested in a peaceful settlement now and were pinning their hopes on a military solution to end the war before the 1968 elections."

A June 1966 Gallup poll cited by Brian VanDeMark in his book *Road to Disaster* showed that support for the U.S. role in Vietnam had fallen by 20 percent over the previous year, to 47 percent, while opposition had nearly doubled to 35 percent. "And 66 percent of the country," VanDeMark writes, "said they had lost confidence in Johnson's leadership on Vietnam. Johnson privately called the results 'disastrous.'"

A CIA appraisal of the effect of Rolling Thunder's impact after a full year of the bombing campaign said that for all its thousands of sorties against military and economic targets, the "resulting damage was relatively light, in good measure reflecting the restricted nature of the air campaign." Over the next year, the bombing restraints would become a major factor in applying pressure to Johnson, as hawks in Congress and at the Pentagon were demanding ever more escalation.

Even though McNamara was skeptical about the efficacy of air power to achieve the administration's goals in Vietnam, and even though he despaired privately over the political situation—which were the subjects of regular discussion in newspaper columns and at Georgetown dinner parties—he became the focus of criticism from inside the administration and in Congress, as the publicly identified architect of a war he himself thought was being lost. McNamara, it was believed, was trying to have it both ways.

The deployment of more troops, the extension of the bombing, the failure to make any headway on negotiations, the hardliners in ascendency in Washington and Hanoi, continuing political disarray, disaffection and corruption in South Vietnam—all these factors made 1966 the year that the United States went all in on the war and also the year when the template for failure in the years ahead was set.

Chapter Five
The Breaking Point

★ ★ ★

AT 7:10 P.M. ON JANUARY 3, 1967, National Security Adviser Walt Rostow signed off on a memo to the president classified "Literally Eyes Only," in which he forwarded what he considered an "improbable" scenario.

"While recognizing all the reasons Hanoi might wish to sweat us out though 1968, I have come to believe it is conceivable if not probable that they are trying to get out of the war but don't know how ... ," he wrote. "I mean they cannot openly negotiate with us. They must have a deal which saves them minimal face with the NLF [Vietcong] and the Chinese to announce before negotiations are acknowledged ... Be clear, I don't give this very high odds, but I have had the nagging feeling they could well be a position of wanting to get out ... I can even reconstruct the reasons for this view," which apparently were based on hints that the leadership in Hanoi was not as united as it once was—wishful thinking, it turned out.

Rostow then outlined a complex set of actions and

responses in which intermediaries would open a secret channel for negotiations with the North Vietnamese.

Nothing came of this ploy and similar feints in 1967. One reason was that Rostow believed then, and to the end of the war and beyond, that the United States would prevail if it showed the determination and provided the resources. Memos were circulated (sometimes selectively in fierce backchannel rivalries), military recommendations were made and debated, and top-level Tuesday lunches were held. A congressional investigation that summer made the case that bombing was being restricted and made out McNamara to be the focus of resistance, which he was.

McNamara's opposition to unrestricted bombing was personal and largely on strategic grounds. Having been part of a bomb planner group in World War II, McNamara believed—as he later told Errol Morris in *The Fog of War*—that he agreed with Curtis LeMay that both could have been tried as war criminals if the United States had lost the war because of the scale of civilian death he and others were responsible for in Japan and Germany. The limitations of air power was one of the factors in his belief that no matter what was being said publicly about military progress and no matter what Westmoreland's kill ratios showed, the war was not being won.

American power—short of using nuclear weapons—just could not offset South Vietnamese disarray and North Vietnamese determination.

The emerging disagreement between LBJ and

McNamara over war strategy also may have had an essentially unacknowledged Kennedy component. Incidents that McNamara recounted in *In Retrospect* and emphasized in the editorial transcripts highlight this.

"Bobby had grown to be one of my best friends," McNamara writes. "When I first met him, he had seemed a rough, tough character who believed that in politics the end justifies the means. But during the eight years I knew him, he grew thirty years in terms of his values and understanding of the world." As for Jackie, as he always called her, she "did not represent the same political threat to the president as Bobby, but she thought no less deeply than her brother-in-law about the issues of the day."

Once, when Marg was traveling, McNamara went to New York for dinner with Jackie, and he recalled that in her apartment "she became so tense she could hardly speak. ... She turned and began, literally, to beat on my chest, demanding that I do something to stop the slaughter!'"

On the subject of Jackie, McNamara spoke to his editors of two episodes that are revealing and colorful. They also show the intensity of her feelings as the war progressed.

Marg was out, and I went up there [New York], and I always—I think I probably went up commercial air. I never had security agents, and once in a while I used a government plane, in which case I would pay the commercial price ... I stayed at the River Club and Jackie was up on 85th ... There was a taxi strike, so I thought, "What the hell? Well, I'll go on the bus."

So I didn't know anything about Manhattan ... I got on

the bus. And it wasn't too full, even in the midst of the taxi strike ... We get up to 85th or wherever the bus stopped ... so I go to the back of the bus to get out of the back door ... The woman in front of me caught her heel in the step and stopped suddenly, and I bumped up against her, and the guy behind me bumped up against me.

Editor: *These people did not recognize you as the secretary of defense?*

McNamara: *Oh hell no. And I'm walking along ... I walked on about fifty steps and I thought, "My god, something's missing." I reached in my pocket, my wallet was gone.*

Somehow, the evening unfolded, because at the restaurant, La Caravelle, McNamara seated Jackie, encountered a friend, whispered his problem, and borrowed enough money to pay for dinner and to fly back to Washington.

On another visit, in the Kennedy apartment, *We were talking about the war and she got so tense she could hardly speak. She was just obsessed with the killing that was going on.*

And then, said McNamara, Jackie, sitting next to him on a couch, started pounding her fists on his chest, demanding he do something.

Summarizing their relations, McNamara said, *She was a much more sensitive person than many people. She was not only glamorous—she was glamorous—but she was a much more sensitive person.*

(Whispers that McNamara and Jackie's relationship might have gone beyond friendship never went further, but almost certainly reached Johnson.)

Another episode in early 1967 happened when Robert Kennedy, now a U.S. senator, traveled to Paris and returned with what to him, McNamara recalls, was "a legitimate North Vietnamese peace feeler." The story appeared in *Newsweek*. When Johnson next met with Bobby, the president—convinced that the leak had been a deliberate ploy by Kennedy—said: "The war will be over this year, and when it is, I'll destroy you and every one of your dove friends. You'll be dead politically in six months."

In his source notes for *In Retrospect*, McNamara writes, "Robert Kennedy reported this episode to me."

Reflecting perhaps his own political naivete, McNamara insisted that "Johnson accepted my closeness to the Kennedys because he understood my loyalty to the presidency and to him. This was even true when he and I split irreconcilably over Vietnam." Lady Bird's diaries support the view that LBJ's warm feelings for McNamara were genuine, but by the end of 1967 Johnson wanted to get rid of his secretary of defense.

Clark Clifford was also very close to the Kennedys, having represented Jackie in personal issues after the assassination—which he refused to discuss with his editors as he worked on his memoirs. How this would have affected his dealings with LBJ is a mystery of personality that probably had more to do with these relationships than it is possible to discern from words and assertions alone.

Clifford's dignified, soothing mannerisms were always an asset to him in his dealings with people, including

Johnson. In more than one instance, Clifford would assure LBJ that he had spoken to Bobby and could report that Kennedy would not actively undermine Johnson, when in fact he was determined to do so.

McNamara's intensity and his publicly bumptious certainty meant that he was always in the limelight and assertive in making a case, even when he knew—increasingly—that it was wrong. This was the perception of McNamara that defined his lasting reputation.

In March, Douglas Kiker, the Washington columnist for *The Atlantic Monthly*, wrote a profile called "The Education of Robert McNamara," which was especially colorful and insightful about the man he called the "second most powerful ... and second most controversial" man in Washington.

"Washington reporters are sharply divided in their opinion of him," Kiker reported. "Liberal columnists admire him and defend him. 'He's the biggest dove in the higher echelons of the Johnson Administration,' says one. "He resisted the bombing of North Vietnam to the very end. He was chief advocate of the 1965 bombing pause. And he's been arguing ever since that the bombing is not doing what it's supposed to do. He's dying to get this war over with."

Pentagon reporters, Kiker went on, had a different opinion. "'McNamara is a great national asset, but so is the hydrogen bomb,' says one. 'Both of them must be utilized—and contained. He has a basic disregard for people.

He has a contempt for the press and the people's right to know. He's very authoritarian." Kiker observed that "the biggest complaint is that McNamara has deliberately misled the press—and through them the American people—on Vietnam: that by imposing secrecy and juggling facts and figures, he has obscured the true facts concerning both the progress and the cost of the war."

Kiker makes a list: In January 1962 McNamara described the situation in Vietnam as "encouraging." In September 1963 it was "getting better and better." In March 1964 it had "significantly improved." In May, "excellent progress was being made." By November 1965, the "United States had stopped losing the war." By July 1966, he was "cautiously optimistic."

This portrait of McNamara once again captures a central reason for the way history has framed the principals responsible for the war: Johnson, McNamara, Bundy, Rusk, Westmoreland, among others, collectively David Halberstam's "the best and the brightest." Their personalities were instrumental in apportioning blame for the debacle.

LBJ as president, was inevitably at the center—he was intense, volatile, and politically manipulative, whereas JFK had been, cool, young, and martyred. And because of his death, how President Kennedy would have dealt with the war can only be an unresolved question.

McNamara's larger-than-life persona and his tendency to relate better to the swells than the hoi polloi was a paradox. He prided himself on being a social iconoclast who lived in Ann Arbor rather than the Detroit suburbs where other auto industry big shots resided. He was an outdoorsman but was always comfortable with Washington's elites—Katharine Graham, the publisher of the *Washington Post* and a social arbiter in the capital, was one of his closest friends and he was always welcome in her circle, even among those who considered his role in Vietnam reprehensible. This remained true years later when I worked with him on his books. A C-SPAN video of a book party for McNamara in 1999, hosted by Katharine Graham for another of his books, *Argument Without End*, about his post-war meetings with the Vietnamese communists, featured a cross-section of political figures and journalists, even as many of these people considered McNamara responsible for the Vietnam war's mayhem.

As 1967 unfolded, the stress of hard work—McNamara's growing sense of the war's inescapable trajectory, his differences with the Joint Chiefs on policy especially over bombing, Marg's and Craig's ulcers, and the pressure LBJ put on himself and others—all this was becoming visible. *In Retrospect* quotes a diary entry by David Lilienthal, a former chairman of the Atomic Energy Commission, saying that he had seen "a harassed and puzzled look in the no longer sprightly" secretary of defense.

Brian VanDeMark's description of McNamara is especially vivid: "The intense strain of professional obligation and the agony born of guilt and destroyed illusions erupted to the surface in sudden and unexpected emotional outbursts," he writes. *"Jesus, it was an unbelievably stressful environment,"* McNamara told VanDeMark and his editors. He was not the only official so affected. In *In Retrospect*, McNamara adds that Dean Rusk—whose stoic composure was a mask for his inner tensions and troubles within his family—would later write that he took to surviving on a diet of "aspirin, scotch, and four packs of Larks," a brand of filtered cigarettes.

The transcripts of editorial sessions for *In Retrospect* convey the major shifts in mood through accounts of how memos came to be written, usually formal in style but generally clear in message. For every memo McNamara would share with the editors, we would urge him to describe the circumstances that led to them. The McNamara-Bundy "Fork in the Road" memo of January 1965, for example, had been a template for escalation after the circumspection of 1964.

Just as significant was a memo that McNamara sent to LBJ on May 19, 1967, his first written break with the president—which he may not have himself recognized was happening. The memo was lengthy, but its ultimate judgment came through unmistakably:

> The memorandum is written at a time when there appears to be no attractive course of action ...
>
> The Vietnam war is unpopular in this country ...

> The Army of South Vietnam is tired, passive and accommodation prone ...
> Hanoi's attitude toward negotiations has never been soft nor open-minded....

And then the peroration:

> There may be a limit beyond which many Americans and much of the world will not permit the United States to go. The picture of the world's greatest superpower ... trying to pound a tiny backward nation into submission on an issue whose merits are hotly disputed, is not a pretty one ...

McNamara came down firmly against General Westmoreland's latest recommendation of deploying as many as 200,000 additional American troops. "The war in Vietnam," McNamara wrote, "is acquiring a momentum of its own that must be stopped." Westmoreland's request, he added, "could lead to a major national disaster."

The reaction of Walt Rostow and others in war councils to the memo, McNamara reports, was "dangerously strong." Whatever McNamara may have thought and argued over the coming months, the war would continue for six more years and spread to Cambodia.

"Could I have handled the issues confronting us with less pain to the president and, most of all, with greater effect in shortening the war?" McNamara asks in *In Retrospect*. "I now believe I could have had and should have. I did not see how to do so at the time."

Lady Bird's diaries reflect how LBJ was faring during this tumultuous year. She wrote in September 1967: "I simply did not want to face another campaign, to ask anybody for anything. Mainly the fear that haunts me is that if Lyndon were back in office for a four-year stretch—beginning when he was sixty years old—that bad health might overtake him ... A physical or mental incapacitation would be unbearably painful for him to recognize, and for me to watch."

The war was also seriously affecting LBJ's Great Society initiatives; the scale of urban rioting that was sweeping the country was a clash between the promises of change and the realities of day-to-day life. The identification of Johnson with so much violence abroad and at home, instead of progressive reform, was emotionally devastating to him, Lady Bird could see the emotional damage, but she also knew that the only way to upend the narrative would be for Johnson not to run again. Her fervent and repeated hope that LBJ would make that decision was the theme that made her diaries so poignant to read years later.

While Vietnam was always at the center of events, the world continued to spin into trouble. In June 1967, a major war erupted between several Arab states and Israel, which Israel, to the astonishment of all, managed to win in six days. Israel's seizure of Arab territories forever shifted the power dynamics in the region. The Six-Day War also turned the Middle East into another front for Cold War military and political competition between the United States and the Soviet Union. In 1973, during the Yom Kippur War, U.S. forces went on high-level alert for direct conflict with the Soviets—a moment echoing the sense of possible conflagration in the 1962 Cuban missile crisis. Decades later, long after the Soviet Union has disappeared, the conflict continues to resonate with shifting priorities that at times have been exceptionally dangerous to the Washington-Moscow balancing act.

Both Robert McNamara and Anatoly Dobrynin credit the "hotline" that was put in place after the Cuban missile crisis with providing a means of useful communications during the 1967 Middle East war and thereafter that prevented Arab-Israeli fighting from instigating direct superpower confrontation. "The episode," McNamara concludes in *In Retrospect*, reflects "how delicate U.S.-Soviet relations remained around the world in the midst of the Cold War. It partially explains the [Joint] chiefs' feelings about the necessity of 'prevailing' in Indochina. And it illustrates the numerous other pressing issues that prevented us from devoting full attention to Vietnam."

Soviet-Israeli ties were broken during the 1967 war and remained fraught thereafter because of the tangled issues around immigration of Soviet Jews and the complexities of the USSR's support for Arab hostility to Israel amid the continuing upheavals in the Middle East. Restoring relations in the mid-1980s, Dobrynin writes, "essentially amounted to admitting that the Soviet Union made a mistake by breaking them in 1967."

In June, shortly after the Arab-Israeli war, Lyndon Johnson and Soviet Premier Alexei Kosygin met in Glassboro, New Jersey, notable as another occasion when the two superpowers grappled for a way to offset their opposing alliances in war zones, with the recognition that war between them could lead to global annihilation. Dobrynin writes that the positions of the U.S. and North Vietnam were fundamentally incompatible, so the sides "seemed locked in a tragic spiral, although I was able to encourage important military limits to it: I raised the issue of atomic warfare in Vietnam, and I was assured by ... the president's entourage that Johnson had completely ruled out the use of tactical nuclear weapons or an invasion of North Vietnam. Moscow knew about these private assurances although they were never made officially."

This tacit restraint by the Americans on how far to go against the Vietnamese communists added another aspect to the many controversies about the U.S. role in Vietnam, and increasingly about McNamara's place in shaping it.

Another benchmark of the Vietnam era was what became known as the "Pentagon Papers" after they appeared in *The New York Times* in June 1971. In 1967, McNamara had tasked John McNaughton, the assistant secretary of defense for international security affairs, to prepare a comprehensive "study" of the U.S. involvement in Vietnam. The scholarly term "study" was lost in what became a crisis over the documents' being leaked and subsequently published. They were invariably portrayed as a revelation of secrets rather than what they were, a documentary aggregation of how and why policies were set and decisions made. The Pentagon Papers would show that any grasp of Vietnamese history and culture by the leading U.S. decision makers was too superficial to be useful in deliberations and decisions.

McNaughton was killed in a plane crash that summer, and the project was managed to its completion in 1969 by one of his deputies, Leslie Gelb, who went on to be a prizewinning columnist for the *New York Times*, president of the Council on Foreign Relations, and an acute and acerbic observer of Washington's power struggles. He may also have been one of the very few people who read all seven thousand pages of what comprised the narrative.

Gelb told me—we were friends—that the real revelations in the Pentagon Papers were not state secrets but the scale of ignorance that prevailed at the time. He also said that when he delivered a set of the papers to McNamara's office at the World Bank, one of the very few copies that were produced before they went public, his sense was that McNamara set them aside. Gelb came to believe that McNamara could never bear to read them. Nor were they a major factor as McNamara worked on his memoirs, according to the transcripts of multiple editorial sessions.

One night in 1971, after the papers had begun to appear

in the *New York Times*, Bob and Marg were having dinner at the home of the *Times*'s influential Washington columnist James Reston—another reflection of McNamara's ready acceptance in Washington's inner social circles after his time at the Pentagon. Reston reported that the paper was refusing to stop publication, as the Nixon administration had demanded. The resulting case went to the Supreme Court which permitted publication in the *Times*, the *Washington Post*, and eventually other newspapers as well.

Whatever care may have gone into to the preparation of the papers, all that was publicly absorbed was the scandal, including, according to McNamara, a conspiracy trope that he had ordered the study conducted in order to undermine Johnson's likely reelection campaign in 1968 against Bobby Kennedy. Rather than credit McNamara with the concept of studying history, the papers added another strand to a narrative of failure.

Years later, when the papers were again being discussed, Gelb would repeat that what the papers revealed was not so much mendacity and sinister design but the enormous consequences of U.S. ignorance and mishap. One example he would cite was a letter written by the Vietnamese communist leader Ho Chi Minh to President Truman in 1947 about a possible relationship with the United States. Gelb told me that Ho's letter was waylaid by the CIA and never reached the president.

In any case, the Pentagon Papers added to the overwhelming consensus that was emerging that the United States was doomed in Vietnam because of its self-inflicted blunders and misjudgments.

Johnson sent McNamara back to Vietnam in July 1967 to assess Westmoreland's request for another huge deployment of troops—which McNamara had already said that he opposed in the May 19 memo. In their briefings, Westmoreland and his fellow generals insisted that American strength was turning around the conflict.

Brian VanDeMark writes that McNamara was, if not persuaded, then willing to reconsider the options one more time. The debate over additional deployment ended with a decision to add 45,000 troops. But that moment of optimism collided with demands in Congress for additional bombing, along with criticism, particularly of McNamara, for opposing the increase.

But even as McNamara was subject to criticism from the hawks in Congress and within the Johnson administration, he also had to contend with a growing anti-war movement among younger Americans, during what became known as the "Summer of Love" in 1967. This was followed in the fall by massive anti-war demonstrations at the Pentagon. Meanwhile, on Capitol Hill, McNamara was being subjected to personal attacks from all sides as congressional demands for more air power and other hawkish criticisms were offset by increasingly vocal criticism from doves like Senator William Fulbright.

President Johnson also saw himself as a victim and

complained to Rostow's dovish deputy Francis Bator, as recounted by VanDeMark: "You doves think the pressures on me come from you ... You are all wrong. The *real* pressures on me are on coming from people who want me to go North, mine the harbors, bomb Hanoi, get into a war with the Chinese—they're crazies. That is where the real pressures are. I am the boy with his finger in the dike protecting you doves from the crazies."

VanDeMark continued: "After he finished, Johnson walked around his desk, picked up a bumper sticker, and showed it to Bator, almost with tears in his eyes. The bumper sticker read: 'All The Way With LeMay,'" a reference to the now-retired Air Force chief of staff (and McNamara's World War II commanding officer) Curtis LeMay, who had advocated bombing North Vietnam "back to the stone age." LeMay was extreme but far from alone in urging ferocity.

Policy confusion, work fatigue, family-related distress, and denunciations from Congress and anti-war activists were all grinding on McNamara. The Senate Armed Services Committee's Preparedness Investigating Subcommittee, chaired by Senator John Stennis, held hearings in August 1967 that McNamara described as "one of the most stressful episodes in my life."

How stress so depletes the body and judgment is one of the main—obvious perhaps but nonetheless central—takeaways from the Vietnam-era record of McNamara and

Johnson, the only two men responsible with a documented record that can be fully excavated.

In *Road to Disaster*, VanDeMark describes the mood as McNamara readied himself for the Stennis testimony: "McNamara's opposition to intensifying the aerial assault ... worsened the growing split between him and Johnson. During a Tuesday Lunch on August 8, McNamara opposed the chiefs' recommendation for increased air attacks around Hanoi and Haiphong, saying such actions risked Chinese intervention, threatened to kill hundreds of civilians, undercut the prospect of sparking negotiations, and were certain to inflame domestic protests."

"It doesn't look as though we have we have escalated enough to win," Johnson insisted.

McNamara replied that the heavier bombing "would not necessarily mean that we would win."

Johnson retorted: "We have got to do something to win."

The president, growing impatient, told McNamara that he would face heat at the hearings.

"I am not worried about the heat," McNamara replied, "as long as I know what we are doing is right."

VanDeMark writes: "'It was quite a scene,' a White House aide recalled, both men going back and forth, tempers rising. Finally, Johnson told McNamara, in effect, you are on your own—I won't pull the rug out from under you, but I am not accepting your argument, in just that way, right now."

Describing his testimony, McNamara writes in *In Retrospect*, "I spent all day patiently and systematically ... explaining the inherent limitations of bombing. I said we had learned that no amount of it ... would allow us to win"—except on a scale of destruction and death that would have exceeded Hiroshima and Nagasaki—though he did not say so explicitly.

"The subcommittee issued a unanimous report severely criticizing me for micromanaging the war," McNamara writes.

The committee said: "We cannot, in good conscience, ask our ground forces to continue that fight in South Vietnam unless we are prepared to press the air war in the North in the most effective way possible ... Logic and prudence requires that the decision be with the unanimous weight of professional military judgment."

Immediately after McNamara finished his testimony, VanDeMark continues, Johnson called him and gave him "a full blast of presidential anger," an aide recalled, and Johnson remarked to another aide, "I forgot he had only been president of Ford for one week" before Kennedy had appointed him defense secretary—an exaggeration, although McNamara had only served a month in that post.

Johnson's anger was less about the position McNamara had taken than that he had done it publicly. McNamara had never done that before. And the breach was serious.

McNamara disputes an account years later asserting that the Joint Chiefs had decided to protest McNamara's position by resigning en masse. But, as contentious and divided as the air war debate had become, the record indicates that the major consequence of all the differences was that ultimately it was Johnson who would have had to resolve them in a way that his political instincts and insecurity about being commander-in-chief prevented him from doing.

As VanDeMark writes, "The accumulated anguish, frustration, and pressure on Robert McNamara reached the tipping point in early November 1967. After years of grappling with Vietnam and struggling to make American policy there work—a policy that he, more than anyone else had crafted and managed—the proud, self-assured man who had come to Washington ... believing every problem had a solution, 'finally bit the bullet,' as he later put it, and concluded that the massive American military effort in Vietnam could not succeed."

This was the background for another memo from McNamara to the president on November 1, which went well beyond the May 19 memo in establishing that McNamara no longer could be in a leadership role for the war. He advocated capping troop deployments; stopping the bombing in hopes, at last, of getting into meaningful negotiations with Hanoi; and turning the fighting over to the South Vietnamese—which the Nixon administration would later call "Vietnamization."

In the editorial sessions for *In Retrospect*, McNamara castigated himself for not taking his advocacy to its logical conclusion: a U.S. withdrawal and full acceptance of the reality that had been John F. Kennedy's belief and, at the core, McNamara's as well. The United States could not win a war that the South Vietnamese were unable or unwilling to wage themselves. The Stennis hearings in August and the massive demonstrations at the Pentagon in October (which surprisingly went off without serious violence) framed the situation: Hawks demanding more war, protestors demanding the end.

In the vortex were the president, privately in such despair that Lady Bird's hopes that he would not run again were foremost in her diaries, and McNamara, who could no longer reconcile his role as an adviser to the president with whom he was at a breaking point on Vietnam—the singular link the two men had.

By continuing to present American military force in Vietnam as essential to defeating communism, the fact that vast numbers of civilians and soldiers were being killed was not an argument for accepting defeat. Disputes over tactics and strategy are the narrative texts of memos and the reflections contained in McNamara's memoir, which is why his remorse was interpreted so widely as regret for himself rather than for the war's victims.

So why did McNamara initiate the moves that led to his departure from the Johnson administration?

What was in my mind ... I felt that [Johnson] was not prepared to accept my conclusions which were that we could not achieve our objective militarily, that we would have to change our objective ... I can no longer have influence on him and I no longer, therefore, need to feel that for me to leave is walking away from my responsibility. If I can't be influential and I can't change my judgment on what to do and I can't get him to do it, then I should leave. I mean it's that cycle of judgment.

No American officials were publicly advocating an end to the war for the sake of the lives of Vietnamese people. The case for victory was to preserve the credibility of American power and resistance to communism.

The publication of *In Retrospect* ignited rage because McNamara revealed that he had reached his judgment on the war in 1966 and 1967, but he had never said so in public, remaining silent about the war until his book was released in 1995.

After leaving the administration, McNamara acknowledged, "*I just turned off.*" He rationalized this with the position that he could not publicly challenge his successors on policies that he had been so involved in devising. He could not and would not turn on Johnson personally, nor would he openly dispute the strategies of General Westmoreland and the Joint Chiefs. As Julia Sweig relates in her book on Lady Bird's diaries: "McNamara was being eased out by the president even as the defense secretary felt a growing pull to resign. Still, the Johnsons adored him. Lady Bird had 'seldom felt as sorry for' Lyndon, and McNamara's departure caused 'great loneliness and separation' for them both."

Johnson never responded to McNamara's November 1

memo. He did again convene the Wise Men—the outside advisers including Dean Acheson, Clark Clifford, and now McGeorge Bundy, who, not aware how far McNamara's disillusion had extended, after consideration endorsed staying the course in the war.

But the endgame was proceeding.

Several unseen maneuvers intersected. McNamara showed interest in the presidency of the World Bank, a position that the American president could fill. Johnson, deploying his political touch, brokered the appointment, successfully avoiding the need to confront McNamara directly.

Clark Clifford was then identified as McNamara's successor at the Pentagon, with the handover to happen in the first quarter of 1968.

McNamara's resignation as secretary of defense was announced on November 29, 1967, and he would officially leave the job at the end of February.

In the meantime, all hell broke loose in Asia during January 1968. North Korea seized the *USS Pueblo* spy ship on January 23 and held the crew for eleven months, an excruciating embarrassment.

On January 30, the Vietcong and the North Vietnamese army launched the Tet offensive across the South, which in the tumult seemed an enormous show of force and a display of U.S. and South Vietnamese weakness. That is not actually what it turned out to be—the offensive was repulsed—

but that was certainly the way it looked at the time. At this time of turmoil, the Pentagon was in transition.

The outgoing secretary of defense was widely considered at the edge of or beyond a mental and physical breakdown, and LBJ was equally an emotional mess, which he would reveal in taped conversations and in the misery that Lady Bird witnessed nightly.

It was in a February 5 phone call with the *Washington Star*'s Jack Horner that Johnson vented his frustrations:

"I don't admit this is a communist victory and I don't think anybody but a goddamn communist admits it. That's what I think. And I think they're just using us, just playing games around us. And nearly everybody I talk to tries to find out what's wrong with our boys, our country, our leadership, our men. Our president's a liar, Westmoreland's no good, anybody that differs with them. When McNamara leaves, why he becomes a hero! He was the goddamnnest screwball as long as he's in there."

Chapter Six
Departure and Beyond

★ ★ ★

I N AN EARLY MORNING PHONE CALL with McNamara on January 31, 1968, Lyndon Johnson commented about observing his defense secretary the day before. "I looked at you ... I thought you were so damn tired, you better go home to your wife," the president said.

The Tet offensive was underway across Vietnam. The seizure of the *Pueblo* had happened, and a potential crisis involving possible nuclear leakage from a damaged naval vessel had been resolved,

"The result is, Mr. President, I'm really not up to date on Southeast Asia, I can't tell you anything," McNamara contended.

To which LBJ said, "The closer you get to leaving, the more I miss you and I just ... there's not anybody in this government that can say as much in as little time as you can."

McNamara then went on to characterize what he thought of the Tet assaults:

"I think it shows two things, Mr. President. First, that they have more power than some credit them with. I don't think it's a last gasp action. I do think it represents a maximum effort in the sense of, they've poured on all of their assets, both in terms of personnel and materiel and this will set them back some, but after they absorb the losses, they will remain a substantial force ... it probably relates to negotiations in some way. I would expect that they were successful here, then they'd move more forcefully on the negotiation front and that thinking that have a stronger position from which to bargain."

The gist of the call was that McNamara was still clinging to the hope that negotiations to end the war in Vietnam might be started before he left office, and Johnson wanted McNamara to know how very much he thought and cared for him.

The cascade of events in Asia were leading to two significant dates: February 29, when McNamara would be formally replaced by Clark Clifford; and March 31, when LBJ would declare that he would no longer run for reelection. The emotional toll for both men had been profound, but unlike other political breaks based on policy failure, there was no acrimony or assignments of blame for what had gone wrong, at least to each other.

Reaching the end of *In Retrospect*, McNamara again seeks to justify why he had gone along with—or not gone publicly against—policies he strongly suspected would not succeed:

Many friends, then and since, have told me I was wrong not to have resigned in protest over the president's policy. Let me explain why I did not. The president (with the exception of the vice president) is the only elected official of the executive branch. He appoints each cabinet officer, who should have no constituency other than him ... A cabinet officer's authority and legitimacy derives from the president. It is also true, however, that, because of their frequent public exposure, some cabinet officers develop power independent of the president.

To a degree, I held such power, and some said I should have used it by resigning, challenging the president's Vietnam policy, and leading those who sought to force a change.

I believe that would have been a violation of my responsibility to the president and my oath to uphold the Constitution ...

Simply put, despite my deep differences with Lyndon Johnson over Vietnam, I was loyal to the presidency and loyal to him, and I sensed his equally strong feelings toward me. Moreover, until the day I left, I believed I could influence his deci-

sions. I therefore felt I had a responsibility
to stay at my post.

Lyndon Baines Johnson was as political as a man could be. Every move had a purpose behind it. The sincerity of Johnson's commitments to his domestic policies, and the progress he was able to make, have meant over time that his presidency is regularly reevaluated for its positives—while always requiring that the Vietnam war offset any praise and render him in the end as broken.

Robert Strange McNamara was unsophisticated in his political judgments—which for LBJ meant that his word could be taken at face value rather than as a reflection of self-interest. McGeorge Bundy, by contrast, had just enough cynicism based on his years in and around the Kennedys and the Harvard elite culture to avoid the public aura of infallibility that was McNamara's problem.

The Vietnam partnership destined to fail was a mismatch of personalities—earnestness to a fault for McNamara and a brew of insecurities and political calculations for Johnson.

On February 28, Johnson awarded McNamara the Presidential Medal of Freedom at the White House.

McNamara's description of the occasion is poignant.

For a person whose image is one of
cool efficiency, I become very emotional at
times, and so it was this day. When my turn

came to speak, I looked at the president and began, "I cannot find words to express what lies in my heart today," then could say nothing more as I choked back conflicting feelings of pride, gratitude, frustration, sadness, and failure. Had I been able to speak, this is what I might have said:

"Today, I end 1,558 days of the most intimate association with the most complex individual I have ever known. Many in this room believe Lyndon Johnson is crude, mean, vindictive, scheming, untruthful. Perhaps at times he has shown each of these characteristics. But he is much, much more. I believe that in the decades ahead, history will judge him to have done more—for example, through such legislation as the Civil Rights Act, the Voting Rights Act, and the Great Society legislation—to alert us all to our responsibility toward the poor, the disadvantaged, and the victims of racial prejudice than any other political leader of our time. But for Vietnam, a war which he inherited—and which admittedly neither he nor we managed wisely—we would have been much further along in solving those problems."

The irony of McNamara's feelings about American social distress and Johnson's compassion was that the Vietnamese people's lives and livelihoods were always considered much less important than U.S. objectives to defeat a determined enemy, communists whose elimination was worth whatever the cost.

McNamara's emotional behavior at the White House ceremony was interpreted as a measure of how close he had come to a collapse—the suicide of one of his predecessors as secretary of defense, James Forrestal, in 1949 was invariably cited as a precedent. In the years to come, McNamara's displays of emotion when with friends and at the time his book was published were seen as self-pity for his policy failure rather than remorse for the losses and injuries for so many American GIs and millions of Vietnamese.

Having spent so much time with him as an interlocutor, editor, media counselor and now a biographer of sorts, I think McNamara's regrets were deep and genuine—for the war's pointless violence and his role in them, which undid his belief in his abilities as a person who could manage, lead, and dispassionately advise. And it had hurt his family, especially Marg.

To end his narrative in *In Retrospect*, McNamara quotes LBJ's letter to Marg: "Though our lives will change ... we will not. Lady Bird and I will never change our feelings for both of you. They are lasting in admiration and gratitude. With love."

And so Clark Clifford was handed the chalice. As an adviser to Johnson without portfolio, he had traversed from arguing against escalation in 1965 to supporting the build-up and bombing of 1966 and 1967. He came to the Pentagon at the moment the Joint Chiefs and General Westmoreland were making a case for increasing the U.S. commitment rather than capping it—and accepting it would most likely never succeed, as McNamara had come to believe.

Within a week, Clifford was with Johnson. To Brian VanDeMark and his editors for *Counsel to the President*, he would recount how soon he realized the inevitable, that the goal had to be to bring "this to an end on the best terms we can get."

It was after listening to the generals in his first days on the job that Clifford thought: "Oh my God, this is hopeless. It is absolute folly for us to go on ... I felt so strongly about it that I was not sleeping very well at night."

On March 4, Clifford made the argument to the president, very much the same one that McNamara had made in the months leading to his departure. Johnson had him make the presentation to a group of senior advisers the next day. As VanDeMark writes: "Johnson, tellingly, did not challenge any part of Clifford's analysis, but instead let him make his case without interruption."

On March 31, at the close of a speech about Vietnam, LBJ announced that under no circumstances would he continue to run for another term as president. Instead, he would devote himself to the cause of a negotiated peace. Yet the war went on.

McNamara wondered:

Why didn't he, when he decided not to run, shift [policy]. Damned if I know. Except that he was the kind of a person that never wanted to say he was wrong. Maybe that was an explanation of it.

But Jesus, I'd a hell of a lot rather than said I was wrong than go down in history as a guy that was totally wrong and refused to admit it. And if I had a few months left as president and I could shift course and I'd decided not to run and I was willing to pay the price of being charged with failures and having caused all these fatalities on this, at least I would begin to correct my error before I left ...

He and I had no conversation after I left. We had conversations after I left, but I never discussed that with him. So far as I know, he's never discussed it with anyone.

On January 16, 1981, the McNamaras returned to the White House, when President Jimmy Carter awarded Marg the Medal of Freedom for her work in founding the organization Reading Is Fundamental, a program to encourage disadvantaged youth to read. Marg was at the end of a long battle with cancer and died seventeen days later.

The Vietnam war was long over. Lyndon Johnson had died in 1973. On his first day as president in 1977, Carter had pardoned draft dodgers. Bob McNamara would carry on until he died in 2009, trying to explain himself and also serving causes to restrain the spread of nuclear weapons, deal with global poverty, and engage with his former Vietnamese enemies and U.S. colleagues to understand why the war had been such a disaster.

He traveled the world and arranged meetings in Hanoi and other locales with historians, journalists, former colleagues, and former enemies. He went to Cuba to revisit the Cuban missile crisis with Fidel Castro, among others. He attended conferences and wrote articles for magazines and journals like *Foreign Affairs*. The objective was always the same: to reconsider every strand in order to reckon how all that happened came to pass, convinced that if the history was rendered correctly—the collection of data in its way—better or safer outcomes could be managed.

Epilogue

★ ★ ★

THE WAR IN VIETNAM ENDED formally for the United States with the signing of what was called the Agreement on Ending the War and Restoring Peace in Vietnam, signed in Paris on January 27, 1973. In April, with the last prisoners of war released, the remaining American troops left, leaving behind only a contingent of Marines at the U.S. embassy in Saigon.

The wars in Indochina did not actually end until the spring of 1975, with victories in Vietnam, Cambodia, and Laos for exactly the forces and ideologies that the United States had been there to defeat.

Whatever power and influence the USSR and the People's Republic of China would have in Indochina thereafter, the countries of the region largely evolved according to historical patterns set long before the U.S. military was deployed to the region.

A united Vietnam is authoritarian, nationalist, and generally pragmatic when it comes to its economic development and alliances.

Cambodia no longer has a royal family. But it has a ruler in Hun Sen who came to power in 1985 and has now turned over the role of prime minister to his son Hun Manet. The population exceeds sixteen million—which means that it has recovered from the massacres of two million or more in the Khmer Rouge era, after the U.S.-supported regime was ousted in 1975.

And Laos is a one-party state on the margins of global awareness, notable for the mist-covered mountains where the CIA flew in support of the tribal people in the losing side of the conflict, many of whom have found a home in, among other places, Minnesota, where frigid winters must be a challenge.

As for the United States, the impact of our decade in Vietnam was profound and lasting. America had lost a war in which the country's vaunted eminence had failed, for all the expended effort it was able to make—and notable afterward that the men responsible for it never expressed regret until McNamara did. "Vietnam" is now a synonym for the limitations of American power and the rise of meaningful citizen advocacy for political and social change.

Lyndon Johnson went home to the Pedernales and to the chagrin of Lady Bird and his daughters resumed unhealthy habits for a man with heart problems that doubtless contributed to his death at the age of sixty-four in the same week that the Peace Accords in Paris were signed.

Bob McNamara was a vigorous fifty-one years old when he left the Pentagon. He spent thirteen years at the

World Bank. It was in the early 1990s that we started to work together first on his memoirs and then on two other books, *Argument Without End* and *Wilson's Ghost: Reducing the Risk of Conflict, Killing and Catastrophe in the 21st Century*, a peroration on conflict that summarized McNamara's considered beliefs on war.

It was around that time that McNamara called me to say that the filmmaker Errol Morris wanted to make a film with him to explore his views on war. My reaction was to warn my friend Bob (as he was to me) that Morris's film would probably put him once again in the limelight of vituperation, just as the publication of *In Retrospect* had in 1995.

But that was not what happened.

In the *New York Times*, Stephen Holden's review said:

> If there's one movie that ought to be studied by military and civilian leaders around the world at this treacherous historical moment, it is "The Fog of War," Errol Morris's sober, beautifully edited documentary portrait of the former United States defense secretary Robert S. McNamara ...
>
> Stocky and slick haired, with rimless glasses and a grand corporate manner, Mr. McNamara appears to be an exceptionally articulate, self-confident man who came to this project prepared to deflect embarrass-

ing questions about his personal responsibility for the debacle. While he readily confesses to having made serious mistakes of judgment, he will not admit to any grave moral failures.

The film posters presented McNamara in his raincoat, a solitary figure—an image that I very much recalled myself.

In his 1995 national book tour for *In Retrospect*, McNamara appeared at a packed event in the atrium of Harvard's Kennedy School of Government. He was holding his own until near the end, when a Vietnam vet began to harangue him, and the audience seemed to approve of the protest. With cameras clicking and rolling, McNamara blurted, "Shut up!" There was a gasp in the room, including from me.

The next morning, at about 7 a.m., McNamara knocked on my hotel room door, wearing that tan raincoat he so often wore and gray New Balance running shoes, and he told me he was going to hike (his word) along the Charles River. "I know what makes people so angry," he said. "But I have to do this. I need to talk about the war and its lessons so we can prevent anything like it from happening again."

He continued on his book tour, traveling alone, lugging a small suitcase and wearing that raincoat. We offered him security, but he declined.

EPILOGUE

Another notable moment took place at *Time* magazine's seventy-fifth anniversary celebration at Radio City Music Hall in March 1998. Certain guests were asked to pay tribute to someone they greatly admired. John F. Kennedy Jr. chose McNamara and made this remarkable statement:

> After leaving public life and keeping his own counsel for many years, Robert McNamara did what few others have done. He took full responsibility for his decisions and admitted he was wrong. Judging from the reception he got, I doubt many public servants would be brave enough to follow his example. So tonight, I would like to toast someone I've known my whole life not as a symbol of pain we can't forget, but as a man. And I would like to thank him for teaching me something about bearing great adversity with great dignity.

McNamara was not present. In July the following year, Kennedy and his wife were killed in a crash of a small plane he was piloting.

On July 6, 2009, McNamara died. He was ninety-three. His family sent a note to those who had offered condolences, saying that in accordance with McNamara's wishes, "there will be no funeral or memorial service and his ashes will be placed in Snowmass, Colorado, and Martha's Vineyard." McNamara's widow from his second marriage, Diana Masieri McNamara, eventually interred a portion of the ashes under a large headstone in Arlington National Cemetery.

I wrote at the time, "I can hear McNamara's gravelly voice and picture him waving his hand to lend emphasis to his determination not to be extolled—or denounced by a protestor—at a posthumous event. In different circumstances he might have been persuaded otherwise ... But it would be inconceivable, I suppose, for his survivors to overrule McNamara's fiat that the scattering of his remains be the only ceremonial recognition of his very full, very long, and very controversial life."

Reconsidering McNamara all these years later, in the transcripts of his sessions with his editors, and all the other material in histories, memoirs, and tapes, especially Johnson's, the judgment remains as McNamara himself recognized, that he could never be forgiven for what happened in the Vietnam war, but by facing it so personally and ultimately so openly, he could make a contribution toward preventing it from happening again. Even so, in Afghanistan and Iraq in the twenty-first century, the United States again waged wars with endings that resembled those in Indochina, especially in Afghanistan, and today confronts in China and Russia two great nations that, each in its own way, are dangerously determined adversaries.

Sources and Acknowledgments

★ ★ ★

The contents of this book are based largely on my conversations with Robert McNamara during the preparation of the book *In Retrospect*. Audio from a portion of these conversations recorded on July 18-19, 1994, is available for download at https://gofile.me/6Psdh/u0tEooeA9.

LBJ and McNamara: The Vietnam Partnership Destined to Fail is meant to combine historical research and personal experience that results in a portrayal that is closer to the reality of the subject than either retrospective scholarship or journalism separately would produce. I have listed below the books that were consulted with that objective.

Following this listing are categories of acknowledgments, beginning with work on this project and extending back more than a half century, to the years when the Indochina wars were underway and I observed and wrote about them for the *Washington Post*.

Beschloss, Michael. *Presidents of War: The Epic Story, from 1807 to Modern Times*. New York: Crown, 2018.
------. *Reaching for Glory: Lyndon Johnson's Secret White House Tapes, 1964-1965*. New York: Simon & Schuster, 2001.
------. *Taking Charge: The Johnson White House Tapes, 1963-1964*. New York: Simon & Schuster, 1997.

Boomhower, Ray E. *The Ultimate Protest: Malcolm W. Browne, Thich Quang Duc, and the News Photograph That Stunned the World*. Albuquerque: High Road Books, 2024.

Busby, Horace. *The Thirty-First of March: An Intimate Portrait of Lyndon Johnson's Final Days in Office*. New York: Farrar, Straus and Giroux, 2005.

Califano, Joseph A. Jr. *The Triumph and Tragedy of Lyndon Johnson: The White House Years*. New York: Simon & Schuster, 1991.

Caro, Robert A. *The Years of Lyndon Johnson: Master of the Senate*. New York: Alfred A. Knopf, 2002.

------. *The Years of Lyndon Johnson: Means of Ascent*. New York: Alfred A. Knopf, 1990.

------. *The Years of Lyndon Johnson: The Passage of Power*. New York: Alfred A. Knopf, 2012.

------. *The Years of Lyndon Johnson: The Path to Power*. New York: Alfred A. Knopf, 1982.

Clifford, Clark, with Richard Holbrooke. *Counsel to the President: A Memoir*. New York: Random House, 1991.

Dobrynin, Anatoly. *In Confidence: Moscow's Ambassador to America's Six Cold War Presidents*. New York: Times Books, 1995.

Goldstein, Gordon M. *Lessons in Disaster: McGeorge Bundy and the Path to War in Vietnam*. New York: Henry Holt and Company, 2008.

Halberstam, David. *The Best and the Brightest*. New York: Random House, 1972.

McMaster, H. R. *Dereliction of Duty: Lyndon Johnson, Robert McNamara, the Joint Chiefs of Staff, and the Lies That Led to Vietnam*. New York: HarperCollins, 1997.

McNamara, Craig. *Because Our Fathers Lied: A Memoir of Truth and Family, from Vietnam to Today*. New York: Little, Brown and Company, 2022.

McNamara, Robert S., with Brian VanDeMark. *In Retrospect: The

SOURCES AND ACKNOWLEDGMENTS

Tragedy and Lessons of Vietnam. New York: Times Books, 1995.

The Presidential Recordings: Lyndon B. Johnson. Volume I. Edited by Max Holland. New York: W.W. Norton, 2005.

------. Volume II. Edited by Robert David Johnson and David Shreve. New York: W.W. Norton, 2005.

------. Volume III. Edited By Kent B. Germany and Robert David Johnson. New York: W.W. Norton, 2005.

Sweig, Julia. *Lady Bird Johnson: Hiding in Plain Sight*. New York: Random House, 2021.

VanDeMark, Brian. *Road to Disaster: A New History of America's Descent into Vietnam.* New York: Custom House, 2018.

★ ★ ★ ★ ★

Recognizing assistance and the contributions of other people carries the risk of omitting names that either should be included or expected to be. This therefore is doubtless not everyone—and to those left unmentioned, my apologies.

Among these names, there are those, inevitably, who have died. They are included in memoriam. Hail and farewell!

For this book:

The editor was Paul Golob, who has been doing this sort of work now long enough to be legendary in the craft and to whom my thanks are limitless.

My longstanding colleague Karl Weber, now the proprietor of Rivertowns Books, has published this book with characteristic expertise.

Maryellen Tseng designed the cover and graphic, which so completely captures the message of the narrative, and the interior text.

Charles DeMontebello, the audio editor and producer, assembled the audio that so effectively conveys the process that McNamara and his editors used in shaping *In Retrospect*.

SOURCES AND ACKNOWLEDGMENTS

I have relied on the expertise of the historians Robert Brigham and Brian VanDeMark for accuracy on events and dates. Errors that may remain are mine. The conclusions drawn from the narrative are not necessarily those with which they agree.

When he learned of this project, Robert Caro asked to read it in manuscript as a possible insight into McNamara for his indisputably brilliant biography of Lyndon Johnson.

At Times Books for *In Retrospect*, Geoff Shandler was my editorial colleague and as a representative of the generation that came after the war, provided perspective that was very valuable.

The writer Peter Petre joined us for the last draft, bringing a fresh view and a skilled pen that helped give the book the tone that still reads well all these years later.

The Times Books team, long now gone from our Random House connections, were supportive and most of all proud of the book, despite the criticism McNamara underwent at the time. Our fax machines were humming with what today would mainly be vituperative emails and texts.

In addition to editing the memoirs of Robert McNamara, Clark Clifford, and Anatoly Dobrynin at Random House, Times Books, and PublicAffairs, I was responsible as editor and/or publisher for a number of other Vietnam-related books. Here are the authors: Elizabeth Becker, Malcolm Browne, Ward Just, Wendy Larsen and Tran Thi Nga, Jack Laurence, William Prochnau, Morley Safer, Daniel Weiss.

Philip and William Taubman, two distinguished historians, will be publishing their major work *McNamara at War: A New History* in 2025. It makes substantial use of the material that is the basis of my book, a compliment.

Over the years, friends have deepened my understanding of what happened in the war: Ray Burghardt and his late wife Susan; Frankie FitzGerald, Les Gelb, Jim Hoge, Lien-Hang T. Nguyen, Jim Sterba, I. F. Stone.

SOURCES AND ACKNOWLEDGMENTS

And correspondents who worked in Saigon for the *Washington Post* in those years: Peter Braestrup, Michael Getler, H. D. S. Greenway, Peter A. Jay, Robert G. Kaiser, Lee Lescaze, Thomas W. Lippman, Laurence Stern, George W. Wilson. Charles Benoit and Ron Moreau, the Vietnamese speakers who made it possible for us to travel, and Vu-Thuy Hoang, our superb Saigon-based political reporter.

At other publications, the cohort included Kevin Buckley, Peter Kann, Mark Meredith, Maynard Parker, Jean-Claude Pomonti, James Pringle, Nick Profitt, William Shawcross, Martin Woollacott, and the photographers David Burnett and Mark Godfrey.

Down the hall from our offices at 203 Tu Do Street was the formidable *New York Times* bureau, led by Alvin Shuster and then Craig R. Whitney and a revolving group of superstar correspondents that Shuster and Whitney superbly managed.

The point of mentioning these names is that this project reflects their influence in shaping the sense that I could take on the challenge of explaining the roles of Johnson and McNamara in the war we all saw unfold and end so badly.

And finally, Susan Sherer Osnos, who came to Saigon to work for the Lawyers Military Defense Committee and came home to a career in human rights with the man who, to his great and continuing joy, she married.

And to Katherine Sanford, our daughter, who carries the instinct that enables her to take the eighth-grade class from Lagunitas Middle School in Marin County, California, to Alabama and Georgia to encounter civil rights, another great American issue of that era.

And Evan, who thirty years after his father and mother arrived in Vietnam, embedded with Marines and covered the war in Iraq with distinction that, having been to another war, we could judge.

Whatever else the "American war" in Vietnam did a half century ago, the impression it left was indelible.

Index

★ ★ ★

accidental president, 8, 52
Acheson, Dean, 126
Agreement on Ending the War and Restoring Peace in Vietnam, 137
air strikes
    Dobrynin on halting, 89–90
    Joint Chiefs urging resumption of, 90
    McNamara, R., opposition to, 121
    against North Vietnam, 88–90
    Rusk on halting, 88
    Vietnam war with, 79–80
Alsop, Joe, 98
"American war," 1–2, 9–10, 91
anti-war movement, 119
Arab-Israeli war, 116
Argument Without End (McNamara, R.), 4, 111, 139
Armed Forces of the Republic of Vietnam (ARVN), 40
arrogance, 7
ARVN. *See* Armed Forces of the Republic of Vietnam
assassination
    Connally present with Kennedy, John, 30
    of Diem and Nhu, 43

    of Kennedy, John, 15, 19–21, 32
audio recordings, from Johnson, L., presidency, xv, 4–5, 49
autopsy, 22

backroom bargaining, 79
Ball, George, 57
    argues that bombing won't work, 73
    departure from State Department, 60
    Johnson administration against, 75
    opposition to Vietnam war strategy, 58
    Saigon coup approval of, 43–44
banking scandal, 76
Bator, Francis, 120
Bay of Pigs, 6, 34–36, 46
Because Our Fathers Lied (McNamara, C.), 86
Bethesda Naval Hospital, 22
Bohlen, Charles ("Chip"), 37
bombing campaign, 9–10
bombing pause, 12
Brigham, Robert, xii
Browne, Malcolm, 40
Buddhist uprisings, 40–41, 85, 100
budget and taxes, 49

• 149 •

INDEX

budget meeting, 19–20
Bundy, McGeorge, 22
    Bay of Pigs supported by, 35–36
    Cline's phone call to, 37
    departure of, 94–95
    as Ford Foundation president, 12, 61, 95
    "Fork in the Road" memo submitted by, 9–10
    important role of, 3, 76–77
    Johnson, L., deteriorating relationship with, 81
    Johnson, L., questioned by, 53
    McNamara, R., contrasted to, 7
    on McNamara, R., debate, 11
    as national security adviser, 27
    Rostow replacing, 12, 82, 102
    television debate by, 81–82
    Vietnam abyss failure of, 60
Bunker, Ellsworth, 3

Cambodia, 1–2, 138
Camp David, meeting at, 10, 75, 77, 82
Capitol Hill, 79
Caro, Robert, xv, 4, 24, 53
Carter, Jimmy, 135
Castro, Fidel, 34, 136
casualties, of Vietnam war, 3
Cater, Douglas, 78
CBS documentary, 98
China
    and Indochina, 137
    Indonesia reversal for, 86–87
    People's Republic of, 11
    U.S. power threat from, 83–84
civil rights, 6, 32, 93
Civil Rights Act, 132
Clifford, Clark
    Ball supported by, 73
    Counsel to the President by, xi, 45, 73, 76, 134
    dignified soothing mannerisms of, 108–9
    important role of, 3
    Johnson, L., with, 134
    Kennedy, Jackie, relationship with, 108
    McNamara, R., debating, 10–11
    McNamara, R., succeeded by, 14, 126, 129
    on momentous decision, 74–75
    and negotiated withdrawal from Vietnam, 76
    VanDeMark's analysis of, 134
    on Vietnam war, 14
Cline, Ray, 37
Cold War, 33, 101, 115
Commander-in-Chief, 10, 72
communications, written, 43
communism
    Cold War and defeating, 101
    crusades against, 87
    Tet Offensive and spread of, 126–28
    U.S. not wanting takeover by, 70
    U.S. resistance to, 125
    Vietnam war and, 51–52
    world order strengthened against, 79
Communist Party, 86
confidential agreements, 88
congressional action, 33, 49
Connally, John, 30
Counsel to the President (Clifford), xi, 45, 73, 76, 134
credibility gap, 12
Crile, George, 98
Cuba
    exiles from, 34
    military intervention in, 37
    Soviet Union deploying missiles in, 37
Cuban Missile Crisis, 6, 33, 37–39, 115

INDEX

Daley, Richard J., 26
death
    of Johnson, L., 16
    of McNamara, R., 141–42
Death of a President, The (Manchester), 23, 50
de Gaulle, Charles, 64
Dereliction of Duty (McMaster), 82
DESOTO patrols, 65
Dillon, Douglas, 27
diplomatic approach, 81, 89
Diplomats at War (Truehart), 40
Dobrynin, Anatoly
    on air strike halt, 89–90
    In Confidence by, xi, 87–88, 101
    presidential administrations as measure of service, 87–88
    on Soviet Union, 116
domestic policy, 12–13
domino theory, 11, 45, 86

"Education of Robert McNamara, The" (Kiker), 109
Eisenhower, Dwight, 11, 34, 70
"end justifies the means," 80
equal rights, 93
escalation, of Vietnam war, 2, 9, 77–78, 84–85, 87

failures, of Johnson, L., 16–17
Fall, Bernard, 84
"Five Silent Men" (book chapter), 82
Fog of War, The (documentary), 27, 31, 96, 105, 139
Ford Foundation, 12, 61, 82, 95
Ford Motor Company, 7, 27
foreign policy, 33, 52
"Fork in the Road" memo, 9–10, 71, 73, 112–13
Forrestal, James, 133

Fulbright, William, 13, 35, 46, 102, 119

Galbraith, John Kenneth, 28
gall bladder surgery, 89
Gardner, John, 78
Gelb, Leslie, 117–18
global reconnaissance operation, 65
Goldstein, Gordon M., 36, 53–54, 61, 95
Goldwater, Barry
    Johnson, L., defeating, 9, 67, 70
    as pro-war candidate, 33, 53
Graham, Katharine, 111
Great Society programs
    civil rights triumphs and, 93
    domestic policy through, 12–13
    to enrich national life, 62–63
    founding principles in, 8
    legislation for, 132
    Vietnam war undermining, 80, 114
Gromyko, Andrei, 88
ground forces
    congressional committee on, 122
    U.S. deploying, 10
    in Vietnam war, 73–74
Guns of August, The (Tuchman), 47

Halberstam, David, 2, 110
Hamlet Evaluation Survey, 97
Harriman, Averell, 44
Herring, George, 92–93
hierarchy, understanding of, 8
Hilsman, Roger, 41, 44
history, x, 23
Hoang Van Thai, 92
Ho Chi Minh, 91, 118
Ho Chi Minh Trail, 97
Holden, Stephen, 139–40
Holland, Max, 25

INDEX

Horner, Jack, 127
Hughes, Thomas, 72
Humphrey, Hubert, 10, 72
Hun Manet, 138
Hun Sen, 138

In Confidence (Dobrynin), xi, 87–88, 101
independent power, 56
Indochina, 137
Indonesia reversal, 86–87
In Retrospect (McNamara, R.), xi, xv
   on Bay of Pigs, 34–36
   Cuban Missile Crisis in, 38–39
   editorial sessions for, xii–xiii, 1, 7, 19–20, 22–23, 29–30, 38, 45, 47, 51, 52–53, 56, 57-58, 60, 67–68, 70, 71, 79, 80, 83, 98, 99, 100–101, 106–7, 112, 117, 123–24, 142
   Johnson, L., letters quoted in, 133
   Johnson, L., mutual respect and, 54–55
   Lilienthal quote in, 111–12
   McNamara, R., on policy in, 129–31
   as national bestseller, xiii–xiv
   national book tour for, 140
   on political objectives, 92–93
   on possible replacement of Rusk, 61
   rage ignited by, 125
International Agreement on the Neutrality of Laos, 34
Israel, 114–16

JFK. *See* Kennedy, John, F.
Johnson, Claudia ("Lady Bird")
   diary entries of, 71, 82, 94, 125
   husband's torment from, 4–5
   Johnson, L., comments heard by, 10, 71–72
   Johnson, L., inconsolable, 83

Johnson, L., physical and mental stress concerning, 114
   sleep problems experienced by, 82–83
   Sweig on, 94
Johnson, Lyndon Baines ("LBJ")
   audio recordings of, xv, 49
   Ball against administration of, 75
   as bully, 54
   credibility gap of, 12
   death of, 16
   Kennedy, John, visit planned to, 24–25
   Kennedy, R., dislike of, 13, 24
   Kennedy, R., political rivalry with, 50
   mandate of leadership and, 68
   McNamara, R., war strategy disagreement with, 105–6, 130–31
   misleading citizens, 52
   presidential term declined by, 134–35
   presidential ticket issue for, 25
   public lost confidence in, 102–3
   as Senate leader, 24
   speech by, 93–94
   unhealthy habits of, 138
Johnson Presidency, The (Thompson, K.), 26
Joint Chiefs of Staff, 21, 70
   air strikes resumption urged by, 90
   Bay of Pigs endorsed by, 35
   changes in, 56
   Kennedy, John, rejecting advice of, 39
   McNamara, R., protested by, 122–23
   military leadership failure of, 67–68

Katzenbach, Nicholas, 60
Kennan, George F., 38, 46, 86–87
Kennedy, Jacqueline ("Jackie"), xvi
   at Bethesda Naval Hospital, 22

INDEX

Clifford's relationship with, 108
influence of, 3–4
McNamara, R., growing close to, 7, 13–14
McNamara, R., having dinner with, 106–7
"stop the slaughter" comments from, 106–7
as Vietnam war opponent, 50
Kennedy, John F. ("JFK"), xv, 3
assassination of, 15, 19–21, 32
assertion that he would not "bungle into war," 47–48
Bay of Pigs responsibility taken by, 35–36
funeral of, 23
Johnson, L., on ticket with, 26
Johnson, L., planned visit by, 24–25
Joint Chiefs advice rejected by, 39
Kennedy, R., on assassination of, 19–21
McNamara, R., announcement by, 29
McNamara, R., not qualified and, 28
presidency of, 5–6
public perception managed by, 55
risk avoidance by, 39
Roosevelt recommended by, 29–30
Rusk and dissatisfaction by, 57
South Vietnam's inability to wage war and, 124
U.S. role in Vietnam war from, 6–7, 32, 45–46
Vietnam and Southeast Asia knowledge of, 46–47
Vietnam issues shaping approach of, 34
Kennedy, John F., Jr., 141
Kennedy, Robert, xvi, 3, 92
Johnson, L., detested by, 13, 24
Johnson, L., political rivalry with, 50
McNamara, R., episode with, 108
McNamara, R., phone call from, 19–21
as presidential candidate, 15
Kiker, Douglas, 109–10
King, Martin Luther, Jr., 13, 15
Kissinger, Henry, 3, 16
Korean War, 33
Kosygin, Alexei, 116

Lady Bird Johnson (Sweig), 82
Laos, 1–2, 138
LBJ. *See* Johnson, Lyndon Baines
LBJ and Vietnam (Herring), 92
leadership, mandate of, 68
LeMay, Curtis, 27, 105, 120
Lessons in Disaster (Goldstein), 36, 53–54, 61, 76–77, 81
Lilienthal, David, 111
Lin Biao, 86
Lippmann, Walter, 102
Lodge, Henry Cabot, Jr., 3, 26, 41, 62
Lovett, Robert, 28
loyalty, 50

Maddox (destroyer), 65–66
Manchester, William, 23, 50
Mao Zedong, 33
martial law, 42
Master of the Senate (Caro), 24
McCarthy, Eugene, 15
McGrory, Mary, 6
McMaster, H. R., 82
McNamara, Craig (son), 86, 99
McNamara, Diana Masieri (second wife), 142
McNamara, Kathy (daughter), 99
McNamara, Marg (first wife), 27, 118, 133, 135
McNamara, Margy (daughter), 99

INDEX

McNamara, Robert, xi. *See also In Retrospect*
   Argument Without End by, 4
   death of, 141–42
   displays of remorse by, 96
   genuine regrets of, 133
   Johnson, L., relationship with, 108
   Johnson, L., war strategy disagreement with, 105–6, 130–31
   misleading statements by, 110
   Pentagon reporters on, 109–10
   Presidential Medal of Freedom awarded to, 131–32
   public presentations by, 97
   as secretary of defense, xiii, 2, 7
   troop strength expansion plan by, 77
   as vice president candidate, 64
   Wilson's Ghost by, 4
   at World Bank, 117, 138-39
McNamara's war, 13, 62
McNaughton, John, 100, 116–17
Medal of Freedom. *See* Presidential Medal of Freedom
Meredith, James, 32
Middle East, 115
military coup, in South Vietnam, 41, 43–44, 65
military forces
   Cuba intervention by, 37
   limitations of, 84
   troop strength expansion of, 77, 87, 119
   of U.S., 21, 124
   in Vietnam war, 62, 124
   Westmoreland requesting more, 74
missiles, in Turkey, 39
morality, of Vietnam war, 85
Morris, Errol, 105, 139
   The Fog of War, 27, 31, 96, 105, 139
   McNamara, R., discussion with, 31, 96–97

Morrison, Norman, 85–86
Morse, Wayne, 62
Moyers, Bill, 75
Moynihan, Daniel Patrick, 6

national book tour, 140
national security, 11, 81
   Bundy as national security adviser, 27
   Vietnam war and leadership of, 51
negotiated settlement
   Clifford pressing for, 76
   "Fork in the Road" memo and, 71
   McNamara, R., considering, 13
   Rostow making it easier for, 104–5
   Rusk putting forward, 90
   Vietnam war ended through, 129
New York Times, xiii–xiv
Ngo Dinh Diem, 40–44, 52, 64
Ngo Dinh Nhu, 40–44, 52, 64
9th Marine Expeditionary Brigade, 10
Nixon, Richard, 3, 16, 26, 101
Nolting, Frederick, 40
North Korea, 11, 126
North Vietnam, 8
   air strikes against, 88–90
   diplomatic approach to, 81
   LeMay on bombing, 120
   political strategy of, 91–92
   Rostow on, 100
   secret negotiation channel for, 104–5
   South Vietnam entered by, 71
   South Vietnam's harassment of, 65–66
   U.S. incompatible position with, 116
   U.S. negotiations with, 11–12
   Vietnam war negotiations by, 112–13
nuclear weapons, 12, 116, 136

Oswald, Lee Harvey, 23

INDEX

Passage of Power, The (Caro), 53
Pentagon
    budget meeting for, 19–20
    McNamara, R., and reporters from, 109–10
    McNamara, R., sleeping at, 38
Pentagon Papers, 15–16, 116–18
People's Republic of China. *See* China
personal doubt, 28–29
personalities, in Vietnam war escalation, 2, 9, 77–78, 84–85, 87
Peter Osnos' Platform (newsletter), xvi
Plan 34A operation, 65–66
policy issues, 31
    Bundy defending, 81–82
    domestic, 12–13
    foreign, 33, 52
    McNamara, R., on, 129–31
policy makers, 3–4
politics
    as enemy of strategy, 54
    In Retrospect objectives in, 92–93
    McNamara, R., affiliations in, 7
    McNamara, R., issue management in, 31
    North Vietnam's strategy in, 91–92
    rivalries in, 50
    Saigon situation in, 44–45
    savvy in, 55
    strategy in, 67
    Vietnam's situation in, 8–9, 103
Possible "Fall-back" Plan, 100
poverty, 136
presidency
    accidental, 8
    audio recordings of, xv, 4–5, 49
    candidates for, 15
    elections for, 52, 70
    issues being presented to, 58
    Johnson, L., in, 26
    of Kennedy, John, 5–6
    term of, 134–35
    ticket for, 25
    vice president excluded by, 72
Presidential Medal of Freedom, 131–32, 135
Presidential Recordings (Holland), 25
pro-war candidate, 33, 53
public perception
    Johnson, L., leadership and, 102–3
    Kennedy, John, managing, 55
    Senate hearings influencing, 102
Pueblo (spy ship), 126, 128

racial integration, 6
Reading Is Fundamental, 135
regrets, genuine, 133
remorse, displays of, 96
Republican Party, 33
Reston, James, 118
risk avoidance, 39
Road to Disaster (VanDeMark), xii, 102, 121
Rockefeller, Nelson, 33
Rolling Thunder bombing campaign, 7, 9–10, 103
Roosevelt, Franklin D., Jr., 29–30
Rostow, Walt
    Bundy replaced by, 12, 82, 102
    on "Fork in the Road" memo, 113
    negotiations plan from, 104–5
    on North Vietnam, 100
Ruby, Jack, 23
Rusk, Dean, 3, 22, 56
    air strike halt suggested by, 88
    Bay of Pigs supported by, 35
    as great American, 60
    "I must resign" comment by, 59
    In Retrospect on replacing, 61
    issues brought to president and, 58

INDEX

McNamara, R., called by, 58–59
McNamara, R., negative portrayal of, 57
negotiation program from, 90
optimism about Vietnam war, 100–101
as secretary of state, 26, 44

Saigon, 9
  military coup in, 43–44
  political situation in, 44–45
Salinger, Pierre, 56
Schlesinger, Arthur, Jr., 56
secretary of defense
  McNamara, R., as, xiii, 2, 7
  McNamara, R., doing duty as, 16–17
  qualifications assumed as, 28–29
  Shriver offering position to McNamara, R., 28
secretary of the navy, 29
secretary of state, 26, 44
self-confidence, 53
self-immolation, 85
Senate Armed Services Committee, 120–22
Senate hearings, 102
Senate leader, 24
Shandler, Geoff, xiii
Shriver, Sargent, 28
Six-Day War, 114–15
sleep problems, 82–83
Sorensen, Ted, 49, 56
Southeast Asia, 128
South Vietnam
  disarray of, 105
  fighting capability of, 69, 124
  Kennedy, John, on inability to wage war of, 124
  North Vietnam entering, 71
  North Vietnam harassed by, 65–66

people from, 63
Soviet Union
  Cuba with missiles from, 37
  Dobrynin on, 116
  U.S. agreements with, 88
  U.S. power threat from, 83–84
  U.S. relations with, 101, 115
State Department, 60
Stennis, John, 120–21
Stennis hearings, 124
Stone, I. F., xi, 84
"stop the slaughter" comment, 106–7
Substack, xvi
Suharto, 86
Summer of Love, 119
Supreme Court, 118
Sweig, Julia
  on Johnson, C., 94
  Lady Bird Johnson by, 82–83
  on McNamara, R., 125

taxes and budget, 49
tax increase, 55, 80
Taylor, Maxwell, 3, 21, 42–44, 56, 62
television debate, 81–82
Tet Offensive, 15, 126–28
Thich Quang Duc, 40
Thompson, Kenneth W., 26
Thompson, Llewellyn, 38
Time magazine, 141
Tonkin Gulf incidents, 9, 51, 65, 67
Tonkin Gulf Resolution, 67
transparency, lack of, 95
Trueheart, Charles, 40
Trueheart, William, 40
Truman, Harry, 118
Tuchman, Barbara, 47
Turner Joy (destroyer), 66

INDEX

unhealthy habits, 138
United States (U.S.)
    China and Soviet threat to power of, 83–84
    communism resistance by, 125
    communist takeover and, 70
    DESOTO patrols by, 65
    ground forces deployed by, 10
    history shared by citizens of, 23
    Johnson, L., misleading citizens of, 52
    Johnson, L., rejecting combat options for, 63
    Kennedy, John, on Vietnam war role of, 6–7, 32, 45–46
    limited power of, 138
    military coup started by, 41
    military forces of, 21, 124
    misjudgments and blunders by, 119
    North Vietnam incompatible position with, 116
    North Vietnam negotiations with, 11–12
    Soviet Union agreements with, 88
    Soviet Union relations with, 101, 115
    Vietnam, Cambodia and Laos engagement of, 1–2
    Vietnam war all-in by, 91
    Vietnam war casualties of, 3
    Vietnam war commitment by, 9
    Vietnam war failure of, 1–2
    Vietnam withdrawal of, 69
    violence in, 15

Valenti, Jack, 11, 75
VanDeMark, Brian
    on Bator, 120
    on Clifford's analysis, 134
    on Johnson, L., anger, 122
    on McNamara, R., 111–12, 119
    Road to Disaster by, xii, 102, 121

Van Tien Dung, 92
Vietnam. *See also* North Vietnam; South Vietnam
    Bundy as failure in, 60
    Kennedy, John, on issues of, 34
    political situation over, 8–9, 103
    righteous goals for, 99–100
    Southeast Asia knowledge and, 46–47
    today, 137
    U.S. engagement in, 1–2
    U.S. military forces in, 21, 124
    U.S. withdrawal from, 69
    Wheeler's trip to, 62–63
Vietnamization, 123
Vietnam war
    activity increasing in, 51–52
    air strikes underway in, 79–80
    as American war, 1–2, 9–10, 91
    anti-war movement against, 119
    audio recordings on, xv, 49
    Ball opposing strategy on, 58
    bombing pause in, 12
    Brigham's materials shared on, xii
    Bundy defending policy on, 81–82
    Bundy's failure avoiding abyss of, 60
    casualties of, 3
    Clifford on, 14
    communism and, 51–52
    conflicting viewpoints on, 98–99
    could not be won, xvi
    end of, 137
    escalation of, 2, 9, 77–78, 84–85, 87
    Great Society undermined by, 80, 114
    ground forces in, 73–74
    Johnson, L., decisions on, 36–37
    Johnson, L., rejecting combat options for, 63
    judgment errors in, 16

INDEX

Kennedy, Jackie, as opponent of, 50
Kennedy, John, approach shaped on, 34
Kennedy, John, on U.S. role in, 6–7, 32, 45–46
long drawn out, 78
McNamara, R., not forgiven for, 142
as "McNamara's war," 13
military adviser for victory in, 62
military coup in, 41, 43–44, 65
military forces in, 62, 124
momentous decision on, 74–75
morality of, 85
national security leadership on, 51
negotiations to end, 129
North Vietnam negotiations during, 112–13
partnership of choices in, 3
personalities involved in escalating, 2, 9, 77–78, 84–85, 87
poor management of, 132
progress measured in, 97–98
public opposition to, 99
Rolling Thunder bombing campaign in, 7, 9–10, 103
Rusk arguing cannot succeed in, 100–101
setbacks in, 15
tax increase financing buildup in, 55, 80
Tet Offensive in, 126–28
Tonkin Gulf Resolution and, 67
two options for, 69
U.S. all-in on, 91
U.S. casualties in, 3
U.S. commitment to, 9
U.S. failure in, 1–2
U.S. ground forces deployed in, 10
Westmoreland's expansion plan for, 10–11, 77, 87, 119

violence, in U.S., 15
Vo Nguyen Giap, 92
vote count, 55
Voting Rights Act, 132

Wallace, Mike, 98–99
Warren, Earl, 49
Westmoreland, William
    additional troops requested by, 74
    conflicting viewpoints from, 98–99
    documentary accusing lying by, 98
    important role of, 3
    McNamara, R., against, 113
    Vietnam war expansion plan by, 10–11, 77, 87, 119
Wheeler, Earle ("Bus"), 62–63
White House
    Bundy's departure from, 94–95
    Bundy's role in, 76–77
    McNamara, R., emotional behavior in, 133
Whiz Kids, 27
Wilson's Ghost (McNamara, R.), 4, 139
Wise Men, 11, 28, 126
women, as policy makers, 3–4
written communications, 43

Yom Kippur War, 115

About the Author

★ ★ ★

Peter L. W. Osnos is the author of *An Especially Good View: Watching History Happen*, the coauthor of *Would You Believe ... The Helsinki Accords Changed the World?* and the editor of *George Soros: A Life in Full*. He is the founder of the publishing house PublicAffairs and a former publisher of the Times Books imprint at Random House, where he was previously a senior editor and associate publisher.

Prior to his career in book publishing, he spent eighteen years at the *Washington Post*, where he was a correspondent in Saigon, Moscow, and London and served as foreign editor and national editor. He is a graduate of Brandeis University and the Columbia School of Journalism, and his writing has appeared in *The Atlantic*, *Foreign Affairs*, and *Columbia Journalism Review*, among other publications. He lives in New York City.